Not So Weird After All

This is the first book to fully examine, from an evolutionary point of view, the association of social status and fertility in human societies before, during, and after the demographic transition.

In most nonhuman social species, social status or relative rank in a social group is positively associated with the number of offspring, with high-status individuals typically having more offspring than low-status individuals. However, humans appear to be different. As societies have gotten richer, fertility has dipped to unprecedented lows, with some developed societies now at or below replacement fertility. Within rich societies, women in higher-income families often have fewer children than women in lower-income families.

Evolutionary theory suggests that the relationship between social status and fertility is likely to be somewhat different for men and women, so it is important to examine this relationship for men and women separately. When this is done, the positive association between individual social status and fertility is often clear in less-developed, pre-transitional societies, particularly for men. Once the demographic transition begins, it is elite families, particularly the women of elite families, who lead the way in fertility decline. Post-transition, the evidence from a variety of developed societies in Europe, North America, and East Asia is that high-status men (particularly men with high personal income) do have more children on average than lower-status men. The reverse is often true of women, although there is evidence that this is changing in the Nordic countries. The implications of these observations for evolutionary theory are also discussed.

This book will be of interest to students and researchers in the social sciences with an interest in evolutionary sociology, evolutionary anthropology, evolutionary psychology, demography, and fertility.

Rosemary L. Hopcroft is Professor Emerita of Sociology at the University of North Carolina at Charlotte, U.S. She has published widely in the areas of evolutionary sociology and comparative and historical sociology in journals including the *American Sociological Review*, *American Journal of Sociology*, *Social Forces*, *Evolution and Human Behavior*, and *Human Nature*. She is the author of *Evolution and Gender: Why It Matters for Contemporary Life* (Routledge, 2016), editor of *The Oxford Handbook of Evolution, Biology, and Society* (2018), and co-author of *The Handbook of Sex Differences* (2023).

Martin Fieder is Associate Professor of Evolutionary Demography at the University of Vienna, Austria. He works in the field of evolution, fertility, social status, religion, and behavioral genetics. He has published in the field of evolutionary anthropology, evolutionary demographics, and behavior genetics in a wide range of international journals such as *Evolution and Human Behavior, Proceedings of the Royal Society B, BMC Evolutionary Biology, American Journal of Human Biology*, and *Biosocial Sciences*, as well as in *The Oxford Handbook of Evolution, Biology, and Society* (2018).

Susanne Huber is Senior Research Fellow at the Department of Evolutionary Anthropology of the University of Vienna, Austria. She works on evolutionary explanations of human behavior, homogamy, and early life factor effects and has published in journals such as *Proceedings of the Royal Society B, Evolution and Human Behavior*, and *Human Nature*, and in *The Oxford Handbook of Evolution, Biology, and Society* (2018).

Evolutionary Analysis in the Social Sciences
A series edited by Jonathan H. Turner and Kevin J. McCaffree

This new series is devoted to capturing the full range of scholarship and debate over how best to conduct evolutionary analyses on human behavior, interaction, and social organization. The series will range across social science disciplines and offer new cutting-edge theorizing in sociobiology, evolutionary psychology, stage-modeling, co-evolution, cliodynamics, and evolutionary biology.

Published:

Mechanistic Criminology
by K. Ryan Proctor and Richard E. Niemeyer (2019)

The New Evolutionary Sociology: New and Revitalized Theoretical Approaches
by Jonathan H. Turner and Richard S. Machalek (2018)

The Emergence and Evolution of Religion: By Means of Natural Selection
by Jonathan H. Turner, Alexandra Maryanski,
Anders Klostergaard Petersen, and Armin W. Geertz (2017)

Not So Weird After All: The Changing Relationship Between Status and Fertility
by Rosemary L. Hopcroft, Martin Fieder, and Susanne Huber (2024)

Forthcoming:

The Evolution of World-Systems
by Christopher Chase-Dunn

Maps of Microhistory: Models of the Long Run
by Martin Hewson

Not So Weird After All

The Changing Relationship Between Status and Fertility

Rosemary L. Hopcroft, Martin Fieder, and Susanne Huber

NEW YORK AND LONDON

Designed cover image: Getty Images

First published 2024
by Routledge
605 Third Avenue, New York, NY 10158

and by Routledge
4 Park Square, Milton Park, Abingdon, Oxon OX14 4RN

Routledge is an imprint of the Taylor & Francis Group, an informa business

© 2024 Rosemary L. Hopcroft, Martin Fieder and Susanne Huber

The right of Rosemary L. Hopcroft, Martin Fieder and Susanne Huber to be identified as authors of this work has been asserted in accordance with sections 77 and 78 of the Copyright, Designs and Patents Act 1988.

All rights reserved. No part of this book may be reprinted or reproduced or utilised in any form or by any electronic, mechanical, or other means, now known or hereafter invented, including photocopying and recording, or in any information storage or retrieval system, without permission in writing from the publishers.

Trademark notice: Product or corporate names may be trademarks or registered trademarks, and are used only for identification and explanation without intent to infringe.

British Library Cataloguing-in-Publication Data
A catalogue record for this book is available from the British Library

ISBN: 978-1-032-73257-2 (hbk)
ISBN: 978-1-032-73288-6 (pbk)
ISBN: 978-1-003-46332-0 (ebk)

DOI: 10.4324/9781003463320

Typeset in Sabon
by Newgen Publishing UK

For our children

Contents

List of figures	*x*
List of tables	*xi*
Preface	*xiii*

1	The changing relationship between status and fertility	1
2	Evolutionary theory and the fertility behavior of humans	5
3	Sources of social status across human societies	15
4	Social status and fertility in preindustrial societies	30
5	Status and fertility in Europe and America during the demographic transition	47
6	Status and fertility in East Asia during the demographic transition	55
7	Status and fertility in contemporary transitioning societies	66
8	The relationship between status and fertility in post-transition Europe and America	77
9	Additional factors influencing status and fertility	92
10	Not so weird after all	103

Index	*107*

Figures

3.1 "Pyramids" of lower Austria: burial mounds from the Hallstatt culture. Height presumably indicates social status of local "kings" and "queens" buried in the mounds. On the left, the highest burial mound (15 meters high "gross Mugl" [large mound]), on the right, a smaller one in a village close by. Picture by Martin Fieder and Susanne Huber   22

3.2 St. Stephen's Cathedral in Vienna. Picture by Martin Fieder and Susanne Huber   25

7.1 Total fertility rate by socioeconomic indicators for 97 developing countries in 2015   67

7.2 Total fertility rate of the developing world, by region 1950–2020   70

Tables

4.1 Studies showing a positive relationship between male status
and number of surviving offspring 40
7.1 Total fertility rate per women (selected countries): time series
from 1960 until 2020 for some selected developing countries 68

Preface

In the early 2000s I found some data from a 1994 special module of the American General Social Survey that had information on all biological children for a representative sample of both men and women. Data on the biological children of women are easy to find, not so much for men. Fertility surveys and other social surveys in the U.S. and other countries have long asked women about their fertility, but until very recently there has been much less attention to male fertility. Given this, I was interested in these data on male fertility in particular. I ran some analyses of the relationship between different measures of status (education, occupational prestige, intelligence, and personal income) and number of biological children. I expected to find a negative relationship between all these measures of personal status and number of biological children (meaning high-status individuals had fewer children), and this is for the most part what I found. But personal income worked differently. For women, I found the expected negative relationship between personal income and number of children, but for men I found the opposite – for men there was a positive relationship between personal income and number of biological children. Initially I thought I had made a mistake, so I recomputed the measures and reran the analyses. There was no mistake. There was a positive relationship between personal income and number of biological children for men. I published the analysis in 2006 in the journal *Evolution and Human Behavior*. At around the same time, others, including Martin Fieder and Susanne Huber, found similar results with different datasets and in many different countries. My finding had not been a fluke! That original study of mine, using an evolutionary approach, began a new research program for me. Martin and Susanne have also used an evolutionary approach in their papers, so it was perhaps inevitable that we would collaborate together on this book. For me, this book represents a summation of 20 years of research. In that time, Martin and Susanne have also gone on to further empirically illuminate the relationship between status and fertility and how it has changed over history, including in the recent past. All three of us agree that theory from evolutionary biology has a great deal to add to

xiv *Preface*

contemporary social science, and this book shows why we think this. After reading this book, I hope you will agree with us.

Our research over the last 20 years has relied on publically available datasets. We would like to thank all the data providers who provided so much rich data, without which our research would have been impossible. I would also like to thank my coauthors – it was a joy to cooperate with you on this book. I am grateful to my husband Joseph Whitmeyer for his support and for reading practically everything I have ever written. I am grateful to members of the Biosociology and Evolutionary Sociology of the American Sociological Association for their colleagueship, in particular, Timothy Crippen, Richard Machalek, Alexandria Maryanski, Kevin McCaffree, and Jonathan Turner, among others. I also thank the editor of this book at Taylor and Francis, Dean Birkenkamp, for his support over the years. Thanks to Laura Betzig, whose early work was an inspiration and who gave comments on an early draft of this manuscript. I am also grateful to my children, Mark and Sophie, who have been the light of my life and now have flourishing research careers of their own. In the words of the Nobel Laureate Bob Dylan:

> May God bless and keep you always
> May your wishes all come true
> May you always do for others
> And let others do for you
> May you build a ladder to the stars
> And climb on every rung
> May you stay forever young.

Rosemary L. Hopcroft
Alexandria, VA, August 2023

1 The changing relationship between status and fertility

In 1975, the first salvo of what became known as the sociobiology wars was launched with the publication of E. O. Wilson's book, *Sociobiology* (Wilson 2000). In this work, Wilson suggested that theory about social species that had been developed in evolutionary biology could also be applied to humans. Wilson famously received a cup of ice water over his head at a conference as a response to this suggestion, but it seemed the cat was out of the bag. Richard Dawkins's book *The selfish gene*, first published a year later in 1976, explained for a lay audience the principles of modern evolutionary theory from a gene-centric point of view (Dawkins 2016). This book convinced many that theory from evolutionary biology may be useful in understanding human social life.

One tenet of sociobiology is that in social species, individual social rank or status is usually positively associated with the number of biological offspring. That is, individuals of higher social rank have more offspring than individuals of lower social rank. Research on groups including the Yanomami of Venezuela and Brazil, the Kipsigis of Kenya, and the Yomut Turkmen of Iran published around the same time suggested that this was also the case in humans, at least for humans in preindustrial societies. Both elite men and women in such societies had more offspring than others, although the basis of social status differed in each, particularly for men. For the Yomut Turkmen, it was the ownership of livestock, as men with the largest herds had the most children (Irons 1979). For the Yanomami, for men, elite status came from killing other men. Men who had killed had more wives and more children than men who had not killed (Chagnon 1988). For the Kipsigis, it was the amount of land owned and the size of herds. Men who owned more land and had larger herds had more children (Borghoff Mulder 1987). Another tenet of sociobiology is that there is more variation in number of offspring for men than for women, and there was also evidence from pre-industrial societies that this was the case also (see the review in Betzig 2012). In some societies, the highest status men could have hundreds of children (Betzig 1986).

DOI: 10.4324/9781003463320-1

2 The changing relationship between status and fertility

Then, in 1986, D. R. Vining published an article entitled "The central theoretical problem of human sociobiology" in which he presented the problem that in modern societies the highest status people have the fewest children, unlike in most social species and humans living in preindustrial societies where the highest ranked individuals have the most offspring. At the time the article received a great deal of attention. Was it the case that theory from evolutionary biology applied to our closest relatives in other species, and to people in preindustrial societies, but not to people in rich, industrialized societies? The data suggested this. For example, census data in the U.S. showed that women in the lowest income families had the largest number of children. It also seemed to ring true to many people who had noticed that poor (and usually poorly educated) women in modern societies seemed to have many children, while many better-educated middle and upper class women had few.

So, have modern humans changed the pattern of human history as Vining argued? While the fact that fertility rates in modern societies are much lower than they are in preindustrial societies is indisputable, is it really the case that in modern societies higher-status people have fewer children than lower-status people? In the years following the publication of Vining's article, there were attempts to answer these questions, and by and large the consensus reached was that it was indeed the case that there is no longer a positive relationship between status and fertility in modern societies. The fall in fertility in developing countries associated with the demographic transition ushered in a negative relationship between status and fertility, a pattern that has been repeated in all societies that have gone through this transition. Humans as a species really were, in modern societies, living in a brave new world.

Yet, in recent years, there has been an accumulation of new evidence that calls into question this consensus – not for societies in the process of transitioning from high to low fertility – but for developed societies that have had low fertility for decades or longer. In this book we examine that evidence and find that even in the lowest of low-fertility societies in America, Europe, and East Asia, there is now a small positive relationship between status and fertility in modern societies just as evolutionary theory predicts, particularly for men. People in modern societies are in this respect not that different to their ancestors in preindustrial societies.

The devil, of course, is in the details. What is social status and what does it mean to say someone is high status? In this book we define status as social ranking, with those higher in social status receiving greater deference, more respect, and greater access to resources than those lower in social status. But how is social status best measured in any given society? Given what we know about the past, the sources of social status particularly in more complex societies are often numerous and thus overall status is correspondingly difficult to measure. How is fertility measured, and whose fertility are we talking about, men's or women's? Unless men and women are strictly monogamously mated for life, something that does not always happen, even in

The changing relationship between status and fertility   3

married couples, husband and wife may have different numbers of biological children. We show that when status is measured in ways that are appropriate for a modern developed society and the biological fertility of both men and women is measured accurately, there is now a small positive relationship between status and fertility in modern societies in Europe, America, and East Asia, most notable for men, even as fertility levels at the societal level have become lower than ever before in history and often drop to below replacement for the society as a whole.

To make this point, we begin with a discussion of evolutionary theory and why it predicts a positive relationship between social status and fertility for individual men and women. We examine the different sources of social status in societies at different levels of complexity. We examine the evidence on the relationship between social rank and fertility from nonhuman species, as well as the evidence from preindustrial human societies. A novel feature of this book is that male and female fertility are examined separately, unlike typical practice when examining the relationship between status and fertility (e.g., Skirbekk 2008; Morita 2018). Most previous demographic studies overwhelmingly rely on measures of female fertility and not male fertility, in part because female fertility is much easier to measure than male fertility. Yet, as we show in Chapter 2, theory from evolutionary biology suggests that the relationship between status and fertility will differ for men and women and that the relationship will typically be stronger for men than for women. Thus it is important to measure both male and female fertility, and where possible we do both.

We also examine the process of the demographic transition, or the transition from high fertility rates to low fertility rates. We examine this process in history and in societies currently undergoing that transition. We note how high-status women, particularly highly educated women, lead the way in fertility decline in all societies, both past and present. This makes sense from an evolutionary view, given that women tend to invest more in their children than men do and are therefore often more active in positioning their children in the society of the future, not the past. This tendency creates an inverse relationship between status and fertility that is apparent in all societies that are undergoing or have recently completed a demographic transition. We note how this phenomenon has helped shape the consensus that modern societies are different (the "weirdest" people in the world) and that there is no longer a positive relationship between status and fertility.

We also examine modern societies in more detail. What is the best overall measure of status in a modern society? In what ways are status and fertility related? Does this apply to all modern societies? What is the evidence supporting this? We will also examine how other factors such as religiousness and homogamy influence fertility. Homogamy is the tendency of people to marry people who are somewhat similar to them. As we see throughout this book, status, religion, and homogamy are usually intertwined in human societies. There will also be a discussion of contemporary evidence of the genetic

4 *The changing relationship between status and fertility*

correlates of both status and fertility, and whether there are likely any population genetic consequences of contemporary trends.

This book is organized as follows. Chapter 2 discusses evolutionary theory and its predictions for the relationship between social status and fertility for men and women. Chapter 3 discusses the sources of social status across human societies. Chapter 4 examines the evidence on the relationship between status and fertility in preindustrial hunting and gathering, fishing, horticultural societies, and agrarian societies. Chapters 5 and 6 examine the historical evidence of the changes that occurred in history as societies developed and underwent the demographic transition, or the change from very high fertility rates to very low fertility rates. Chapter 7 reviews the evidence from societies that are currently in the middle of their demographic transitions. In Chapter 8, we examine contemporary, rich, developed nations in Europe and America that have fully completed the demographic transition and now have extremely low fertility rates. What is the evidence for the relationship between status and fertility in modern societies? In Chapter 9, we examine how fertility is influenced by other characteristics such as religion and homogamy. Chapter 10 concludes on the relationship between status and fertility for men and women across all human societies.

References

Betzig, L. (2012). Means, variances, and ranges in reproductive success: Comparative evidence. *Evolution and Human Behavior*, 33(4), 309–317.

Betzig, L. L. (1986). *Despotism and differential reproduction: A Darwinian view of history*. Chicago: Aldine.

Borghoff Mulder, M. (1987). On cultural and reproductive success: Kipsigis evidence. *American Anthropologist*, 89(3), 617–634.

Chagnon, N. A. (1988). Life histories, blood revenge, and warfare in a tribal population. *Science*, 239(4843), 985–992.

Dawkins, R. (2016). *The selfish gene* (Oxford Landmark Science). Oxford University Press; 40th Anniversary edition. ISBN-10: 0198788606.

Irons, W. (1979). Cultural and biological success. In N. A. Chagnon & W. Irons (Eds), *Evolutionary biology and human social behavior: An anthropological perspective* (pp. 257–272). North Scituate, MA: Duxbury Press.

Morita, M., 2018. Demographic studies enhance the understanding of evolutionarily (mal) adaptive behaviors and phenomena in humans: A review on fertility decline and an integrated model. *Population Ecology*, 60(1–2), 143–154.

Skirbekk, V. (2008). Fertility trends by social status. *Demographic Research*, 18, 145–180.

Vining, D. R. (1986). Social versus reproductive success: The central theoretical problem of human sociobiology. *Behavioral and Brain Sciences*, 9(1), 167–187.

Wilson, E. O. (2000). *Sociobiology: The new synthesis*. Cambridge, MA: Harvard University Press.

2 Evolutionary theory and the fertility behavior of humans

Evolutionary theory refers to the modern synthesis of evolutionary biology, which is based on Darwin's theory of evolution and includes later developments, including Bateman's principle (Bateman 1948), William Hamilton's work on inclusive fitness theory (Hamilton 1964), and other updates on the theory of parental investment provided by Robert Trivers (1972). While application of this theory to nonhuman animals is relatively uncontroversial, applications of the theory to humans is almost always controversial as the sociobiology controversy of the 1970s showed. Nevertheless, when applied to humans the theory makes clear predictions as to the relationship between social status or rank and reproductive success (number of offspring) and how that relationship is likely to differ for men and women.

Evolution by natural selection

Darwin's theory of evolution is really two theories – the theory of evolution by natural selection and the theory of evolution by sexual selection. The theory of evolution by natural selection assumes that individuals (of whatever kind) vary in some heritable trait. Some individuals with a particular version of the heritable trait are more likely to survive and reproduce, so that version of the heritable trait is more likely to be reproduced in the next generation. Other individuals with other versions of the heritable trait are less likely to survive and reproduce, so those versions of the heritable trait are less likely to be reproduced in the next generation. Over many generations of this process you end up with a population of individuals most of whom have the version of the heritable trait that, on average, helped their ancestors survive and reproduce in the past. There is no guarantee that this trait will help individuals survive and reproduce in the present or future. As is often said, evolution is a blind process and by its very nature is nonteleological.

Since Darwin's time, we have learned that the heritable material that is passed on through the generations is DNA (deoxyribonucleic acid), and the differences in the versions of the heritable traits are caused by differences in the segments of DNA called genes. The process of evolution by natural

DOI: 10.4324/9781003463320-2

6   *Evolutionary theory and the fertility behavior of humans*

selection can be rephrased in terms of genes, as follows. Genes for traits that help an individual survive and reproduce in a particular environment are more likely to be successfully replicated in the next generation, whereas genes for traits that don't help an individual survive and reproduce are less likely to be replicated in the next generation. After many generations of this process you have a population with individuals with genes for traits that helped their ancestors survive and reproduce, on average, in the past, and in the environments of the past.

This is the basic process of evolution by natural selection; however, it can be complicated by other processes such as genetic drift, where the frequencies of alleles change randomly and not because of natural selection. It is also important to keep in mind that at the genomic level, most traits are polygenic (many genetic loci are influencing a phenotypic trait) and many genetic loci are pleiotropic (a genetic locus is influencing many phenotypic traits), respectively (Mills et al. 2020). As a consequence, selection for one trait usually means that another trait may also be selected for, leading to a by-product of selection. Hence, genes for many traits are not necessarily directly selected for and thus considered adaptive, but may merely represent a by-product of selection for genes for another trait (Relethford 2012; Mills et al. 2020).

It is essential to note that in all species, species-typical traits in current populations represent past, and not necessarily present, selective pressures. It does not mean that those species-typical traits will help individuals survive and reproduce in every environment. Species-typical traits are likely to help individuals survive and reproduce in the present only to the extent to which current environments are similar to past environments. The genes for species-typical traits are much less likely to help individuals survive and reproduce in environments that are radically different from historical environments or in environments that are changing rapidly.

Sexual selection

Reproduction is key to evolution by natural selection, and for individual organisms that reproduce sexually the key to reproduction is finding a mate. That is where sexual selection comes in. Any heritable trait that helps an individual obtain a mate is likely to be reproduced in the next generation. There are two different types of sexual selection that often co-occur – intrasexual selection where individuals of the same sex compete with each other in order to monopolize matings with the opposite sex, and intersexual selection where members of the same sex compete with each other to be chosen by members of the opposite sex (Alcock 2001, pp. 399–404, 434–440).

Intrasexual selection occurs when males fight each other for access to females, as occurs in many species, for example, elephant seals or red deer. Genes for traits that help males win these competitions, gain access to mates, and successfully reproduce are likely to be replicated in the next generation and consequently spread through the population. A good example is red

Evolutionary theory and the fertility behavior of humans   7

deer, a species that has been extensively studied (Alcock 2001, pp. 274–275). Males with characteristics such as large size, large and sharp antlers, a strong neck, and a willingness to fight are more likely to win competitions with other males, and thus accumulate a larger harem of female deer and sire more offspring in the breeding season. As a result, over evolutionary time there has been selection for the genes for size, strength, strong antlers, and aggressiveness in the breeding season in males, and this has resulted in male deer that have those traits.

Intersexual selection occurs when one sex displays itself hoping to be selected by the opposite sex. For example, mates can be attracted by elaborate nest buildings (e.g., in bowerbirds; Borgia 1986; Diamond 1986) or larger territories providing resources needed for rearing the offspring (Reynolds 1996). In the male guppy (Brooks & Endler 2001; Kemp et al. 2009), ornaments and movement quality during courtship help to defend a territory and signal mate quality to attract potential mates. In this case genes for traits that the opposite sex most chooses are likely to be replicated through the generations. Sometimes these traits can in fact inhibit survival – large costly traits such as the male peacock's tail are an example (Catchpole 1987; Zahavi & Zahavi 1999). The large flashy tail of the male peacock is beautiful, but it is energetically costly to grow and maintain and it can attract predators and slow a male peacock's escape, thus making it more likely that the peacock dies prematurely. But as long as the male peacock with these traits survives long enough to be able to successfully reproduce and is more likely to reproduce than other peacocks, genes for those traits will be replicated in subsequent generations and persist in the population.

Any trait indicating mate quality or competitive ability such as songbird songs, mating displays, ornaments, body size, and so on may be also understood in the framework of costly signaling and the handicap principle (Zahavi 1975; Zahavi & Zahavi 1999): the trait is considered a reliable honest signal of quality that is so costly that it cannot be afforded by individuals who are low on that quality. For instance, a peacock in bad condition would not be able to produce a magnificent tail. The tail thus is a reliable indicator of the peacock's good condition and hence its quality as a mate. The female preference for honest signals may lead to an "evolutionary escalating loop" resulting in displays like the peacock tail that are quite detrimental in terms of survival but highly beneficial in terms of mate attraction.

Generally, in sexually reproducing species, it is the sex that invests the least in offspring that is most subject to sexual selection – often, but not always, it is the males (Trivers 1972). So it tends to be the males who are most likely to compete amongst themselves for access to mates, and the males who have the flashy ornaments like bright tails or colorful feathers and elaborate mating displays and other costly signals, and the females are the choosers. But there are some species where the males invest more in offspring than the females. Where the males invest more in offspring, they tend to be the more choosy

8   *Evolutionary theory and the fertility behavior of humans*

ones. For example, in a species of water bird called Wilson's phalaropes, the male invests more in offspring and is choosier about his mate than the female (Delehanty et al. 1998). The female phalarope deserts her mate once she's laid eggs and the male raises the young by himself. The female then goes off to look for other males to mate with. In this species there is intense female/female competition for mates and the females are more brightly colored than the males.

Sexual selection is also influenced by the prevailing sex ratios in the mating population. The sex that is in the majority is the one that is likely to be subject to sexual selection, since they will be competing for mates, and the sex that is in the minority will be the one doing the choosing. However, Fisher's principle (Fisher 1958) means that imbalanced sex ratios are likely to be corrected over evolutionary time by the process of natural selection. Fisher's principle works because in a mating population in which one sex is comparatively rare, any individual with a genetic trait that allows it to produce more of the rarer sex will likely leave more offspring of the rarer sex. These offspring in turn will be less subject to sexual selection and therefore more likely to reproduce, and so the genetic trait encouraging the production of the rarer sex will increase its representation in subsequent generations. After several generations, individuals with this genetic trait will be abundant in the population, there will be consequently greater production of the rarer sex, and soon the sex that was initially rarer likely will no longer be the minority and the sex ratio will be back in balance.

Sex differences in parental investment in humans

Sexual selection typically operates more on males because males usually invest less in their offspring (Trivers 1972). In many species the father's role is limited to fertilization of the female. Humans are unusual among species in that humans have extensive biparental investment – meaning human fathers typically do invest in their offspring. However, in humans as in all mammals, females invest more. First, they have a greater fixed biological investment in the offspring. Women have the larger and more costly gametes – the eggs, and women produce only about 400 viable eggs in their lifetime. Men, in contrast, have gametes that are comparatively tiny and have a trivial cost – the average man produces millions of sperm every day. For a woman, having a child involves at a minimum a 9-month pregnancy with its associated expenditure of physiological effort and energy. In the evolutionary past there was no baby formula or alternative to breast milk, so a child also required an energy-intensive period of nursing for 1–2 years afterward in order to survive. For our nomadic hunter and gatherer ancestors, small babies also needed to be carried from place to place, an additional expenditure of effort typically made by the mother. Yet even without the costs of carrying and nursing that women would have borne over the millennia humans lived as hunters and gatherers, a woman's fixed, unavoidable biological investments

Evolutionary theory and the fertility behavior of humans 9

(the large gamete, and the biological resources and time necessary for gestation) in each child are much higher than a man's.

This larger investment and the limited time that human females are able to bear children mean that the number of children a woman can have in her lifetime is strictly limited. This is much less the case for men, whose fixed investment in each child is tiny and who can father children well into old age. These sex differences are illustrated by the difference in documented fertility between men and women – the man who sired the largest number of children on record, Ismail the Bloodthirsty of Morocco, had at least 800 children, while the woman who had the most children on record, the wife of Feodor Vassilyev of Russia, had just 69 children (Most Prolific Mother Ever, n.d.). These differences mean that each child represents a greater proportion of a woman's potential reproductive effort than a man's. As such, each child is more reproductively valuable for the woman than the man, as each child forms a larger share of her possible opportunities for replicating her genetic material in the next generation.

Because women's fixed biological investment in each child is so large and each child represents a large share of her potential reproductive effort, in the ancestral past women with genes for traits that encouraged them to take care of each child were more likely to leave genetic descendants, and women with genes for traits that encouraged them to not take care of each child were much less likely to leave genetic descendants. As a result, there was likely selection for genes for traits that encourage women to care for each of their children. Since each child is a trivial biological investment for a man and each child represents a smaller share of his potential reproductive effort, this is less the case for men. In the ancestral past, as is the case for women, men with genes for traits that encouraged them to take care of each child would likely leave genetic descendants. However, men with genes for traits that encouraged them to be more equivocal in the care of each child could still leave descendants, in part because the mothers of the children were likely not to abandon the children even if they did. After many generations this leads to a population of men with genes for traits that encourage them to take care of their children, but more contingently, than women. The resulting population has women with genes for traits that predispose them to care for each child, and men with genes for traits that predispose them to make provision of childcare more contingent on personal, environmental, and social factors. That this process has occurred over evolutionary time is demonstrated by sex differences in behavior patterns, as in all societies today and in the past mothers are much less likely to abandon their offspring than fathers.

Sex differences in mate preferences

In the ancestral past, men with genes that encouraged them to pursue additional matings with other women would have been more likely to leave genetic descendants than men with genes that encouraged them not to do this.

10   *Evolutionary theory and the fertility behavior of humans*

This is less likely the case for women, as additional matings are less likely to lead to additional offspring for women given the fixed time and energy costs involved with childbearing for women (Bateman 1948). A man can have twenty mates in a year and leave twenty children, while a woman can have twenty mates in a year and will most likely leave just one or sometimes two children. This means that over evolutionary time, there would have been selection for genes for traits encouraging sex with additional partners in men more so than in women. As is always the case, genes for behavioral traits may predispose individuals to certain traits, but actual behavior is always contingent on many factors, including social and cultural contexts. This cultural and social context can override or accentuate any evolved predisposition. Any predisposition is just that – it does not necessarily translate into behavior. However, greater male interest in casual sex and behavioral differences between men and women with regard to casual sex are widely documented. For example, prostitutes almost always cater to a male, not a female, clientele. The sex difference in interest in casual sex is also nicely illustrated by the Clark and Hatfield experiment (1989), since replicated in other cultures besides the U.S. (e.g., France, see Guéguen 2011), that shows that women are much less likely than men to agree to propositions of sex by attractive strangers than men. In the original Clark and Hatfield experiment, while the majority of men agreed with the proposition, none of the women did.

Because throughout most of human history the outcome of sex can result in a pregnancy for women, women with genes for traits that encouraged them to be choosy about when, where, and with whom they became pregnant were more likely to leave genetic descendants than women with genes that encouraged them not to be choosy. This was less likely the case for men as they pay none of the costs of childbearing and childbirth. So after many generations, there was likely selection of genes for traits that encourage women to be choosy about mates and mating, and selection of genes for traits that encourage men to be somewhat less choosy about mates and mating. This does not mean that men are not choosy about mates – it does mean that women are likely to be more choosy about mates, more of the time than men, on average.

So whom are women going to choose to mate with? In the past women with genes for traits that encouraged them to find a partner who was able to help her and her children survive and thrive in the contemporary environment would have left more descendants than women who did not. Generally, partners with high social status or rank within the group are well positioned to do this, as they usually have greater access to material resources and social support, and so it is likely that women in the ancestral past who preferred male partners with high social rank left more descendants than women who did not, on average. Men with high status may also have genes that helped them attain that status, and these same genes may also help the woman's offspring survive and thrive and likely leave descendants, making high-status

Evolutionary theory and the fertility behavior of humans 11

men even more beneficial as mates. Thus, evolutionary theory predicts that women will have genes for traits that encourage them to prefer higher-status men to lower-status men as sexual partners, on average.

Given female interest in high-status mates, and male interest in additional matings, males with genes for traits encouraging the pursuit of high status will be more likely to both obtain status and find at least one mate and maybe more than one. This will mean males with these traits will be more likely to leave genetic descendants, and so genes for traits encouraging status-striving (particularly in males) will be more likely to be replicated in future generations than genes for traits that frustrate status-striving.

In humans both the mother and father usually provide parental care, albeit fathers less reliably so. Men are more likely to cut short their investment in a child, as we have seen, but men are also likely to invest in at least some of their children. Just as with women, genes for traits that encourage this behavior would have been successfully replicated in subsequent generations. Particularly if they foresee that they will invest in any resulting offspring, men are also likely to be choosy about who their sexual partners are. Given the benefits of social status for offspring, men are also likely to prefer higher-status women for the same reasons women do, all else being equal. But there are limiting factors. Status in many human societies usually increases with age, yet women have a limited time in their life when they can bear children. Because women can have children for only a short span of their life, men with genes for traits that encouraged them to prefer long-term partners who were older than the age of menopause would have left no genetic descendants. Men with genes for traits that encouraged them to prefer long-term partners who were young, healthy, and fertile would have been likely to have left many descendants. So over evolutionary time there was likely selection of genes for traits in men that encourage them to prefer long-term partners who are young, healthy, and fertile. That this is the case is illustrated by the preference for and choice of younger wives or partners by men that has been documented worldwide. For example, a recent study of 130 countries found that worldwide men are an average of 4.2 years older than their wives or cohabiting partners, with the largest gap being 8.6 years in sub-Saharan Africa and the smallest gap being 2.2 years in North America (Ausubel et al. 2022). Even in contemporary societies such as the U.S., there is evidence that a woman's age is inversely correlated with desirability as a romantic partner, yet for men, age is positively associated with desirability (Bruch & Newman 2018).

Further, for men there can be uncertainty about whether their partner's children are in fact their own – this is called paternity uncertainty. There is of course no such thing as maternity uncertainty – a mother always knows a child is hers (or she could until very recently with the advent of assisted fertility technologies). Over evolutionary history, men with genes for traits that encouraged them to find a long-term partner who was likely to be sexually faithful and then be concerned that she remains sexually faithful were more

12 Evolutionary theory and the fertility behavior of humans

likely to leave genetic descendants than men with genes for traits that did not encourage these traits. So the resulting population of males will have genes for traits that encourage them to prefer long-term partners who are young, healthy, fertile, and faithful and prioritize these characteristics over other desirable characteristics such as social status.

Thus, evolutionary theory suggests that women will prioritize status in a long-term mate, while men will be less likely to prioritize status in a long-term mate and more likely to prioritize youth, health, and fidelity. Given this, high-status, resource-rich men are more likely to find and retain long-term mates than lower-status men. Because men do not prioritize social status in a mate, for a woman high social status is less likely to be positively associated with finding and retaining a long-term mate. This predicts a stronger positive relationship between social status and fertility for men than women.

Women and men do not make mating choices in a social vacuum. Every society has social rules that govern sexual behavior, marriage, child-bearing, and kinship. Yet most cultures accommodate sex differences in mating preferences in some way. Further, it is likely that over evolutionary time each individual's relatives also played a role in individual mate choice (Apostolou 2010). This is particularly true in societies beyond the foraging or hunting and gathering level of subsistence. An individual's relatives include genetic kin and also nongenetic kin who share genetic interests, such as husbands or wives who share genetic interests in their joint children. Of genetic kin, each parent shares 50% of their genes with their children. This holds true on average for siblings; they share about 50% of their genes with each other. Individuals also share on average 25% of their genes with nephews and nieces who are children of their siblings and 12.5% of genes with their first-order cousins (Hamilton 1964). Hamilton's (1964) principle of inclusive fitness shows that an individual can increase his or her own genetic legacy by aiding genetic relatives. Individuals with genes for traits that predispose them to encourage their children and other genetic relatives to make choices, including choice of mate, that are likely to lead to successful reproduction can improve their inclusive fitness and thus are more likely to leave genetic descendants than other individuals. Thus, we can expect that relatives will encourage their younger relatives to make mating decisions that will help their genes be successfully replicated across the generations, at least a good proportion of the time. If the younger relative is a male, then older people will likely encourage him to find a young, healthy, fertile, and faithful mate. If the younger relative is a female, then older will likely encourage her to find a committed, high-status, and resource-rich mate.

In sum, theory from evolutionary biology suggests that women on average will be more likely to take care of their children and more likely to be choosy in mating than men. It also suggests that when it comes to choosing a long-term mate, a woman (and her family) will prefer a high-status man all else being equal, while a man (and his family) will prioritize youth, health, fertility, and

Evolutionary theory and the fertility behavior of humans 13

fidelity in a mate over social status. Given this, evolutionary theory suggests that high-status males will be more likely to be selected as mates and more likely to have children than low-status males. High-status females are also more likely to be preferred as mates, but because males are more likely to prioritize youth than status in a mate, the positive relationship between status and fertility is likely to be less for females than it is for males, and may even be nonexistent or negative. Much depends on the nature of status in a society and how it is attained, and this is what we examine in Chapter 3.

References

Alcock, J. (2001). *Animal behavior: An evolutionary approach.* Sunderland, MA: Sinauer Associates. ISBN-10: 1605358940.

Apostolou, M. (2010). Sexual selection under parental choice in agropastoral societies. *Evolution and Human Behavior*, 31(1), 39–47.

Ausubel, J., Kramer, S., Shi, A. F., & Hackett, C. (2022). Measuring age differences among different-sex couples: Across religions and 130 countries, men are older than their female partners. *Population Studies*, 76(3), 1–12.

Bateman, A. J. (1948). Intra-sexual selection in Drosophila. *Heredity*, 2(3), 349–368.

Borgia, G. (1986). Sexual selection in bowerbirds. *Scientific American*, 254(6), 92–101.

Brooks, R., & Endler, J. A. (2001). Direct and indirect sexual selection and quantitative genetics of male traits in guppies (*Poecilia reticulata*). *Evolution*, 55(5), 1002–1015.

Bruch, E. E., & Newman, M. E. J. (2018). Aspirational pursuit of mates in online dating markets. *Science Advances*, 4(8), eaap9815.

Catchpole, C. K. (1987). Bird song, sexual selection and female choice. *Trends in Ecology and Evolution*, 2(4), 94–97.

Clark, R. D., & Hatfield, E. (1989). Gender differences in receptivity to sexual offers. *Journal of Psychology and Human Sexuality*, 2(1), 39–55.

Delehanty, D., Fleischer, R. C., & Colwell, M. (1998). Sex-role reversal and the absence of extra-pair fertilization in Wilson's phalaropes. *Animal Behaviour*, 55(4), 995–1002.

Diamond, J. (1986). Biology of birds of paradise and bowerbirds. *Annual Review of Ecology and Systematics*, 17(1), 17–37.

Fisher, R. A. (1958). *The genetical theory of natural selection.* Oxford: Clarendon Press.

Guéguen, N. (2011). Effects of solicitor sex and attractiveness on receptivity to sexual offers: A field study. *Archives of Sexual Behavior*, 40(5), 915–919.

Hamilton, W. D. (1964). The genetical evolution of social behaviour. II. *Journal of Theoretical Biology*, 7(1), 17–52.

Kemp, D. J., Reznick, D. N., Grether, G. F., & Endler, J. A. (2009). Predicting the direction of ornament evolution in Trinidadian guppies (*Poecilia reticulata*). *Proceedings of the Royal Society B: Biological Sciences*, 276(1677), 4335–4343.

Mills, M. C., Barban, N., & Tropf, F. C. (2020). *An introduction to statistical genetic data analysis.* Cambridge, MA: MIT Press. ISBN-10: 0262538385.

Most Prolific Mother Ever. (n.d.) *Guinness book of world records*, Retrieved September 18, 2023, from www.guinnessworldrecords.com/world-records/most-prolific-mother-ever

14 *Evolutionary theory and the fertility behavior of humans*

Relethford, J. H. (2012). *Human population genetics*. Hoboken, NJ: John Wiley & Sons. ISBN-10: 0470464674.

Reynolds, J. D. (1996). Animal breeding systems. *Trends in Ecology and Evolution*, 11(2), 68–72.

Trivers, R. (1972). Parental investment and sexual selection. In B. Campbell (Ed.), *Sexual selection and the descent of man, 1871–1971* (pp. 136–179). Chicago: Aldine.

Zahavi, A. (1975). Mate selection – a selection for a handicap. *Journal of Theoretical Biology*, 53(1), 205–214.

Zahavi, A., & Zahavi, A. (1999). *The handicap principle: A missing piece of Darwin's puzzle*. New York: Oxford University Press.

3 Sources of social status across human societies

While social status and rank are important and influence mating in all social species, animals as well as humans, the actual indicator of social status may differ according to the species observed, to the context as well as to the culture. In this respect culture is not limited to humans and has been documented, for example, for the territorial songs of tropical sparrows (Danner et al. 2011) and for the songs of whales. Human social status is defined very differently in different ecological, cultural, and historic contexts, and sometimes it is difficult to know exactly which characteristic conveys the most social status in the sense that it is rewarded with the most deference, respect, and access to resources and is most valued by prospective mates. In most human societies there are competing sources of social status. For example, in early medieval Europe, landholding conveyed social status as did high standing in the church, but being a great warrior and conquering and retaining numerous territories trumped both (and could be rewarded with both). Sex itself is a source of social status, as males often have higher social status than females in most societies, all else being equal. The evolutionary reasons for this may be that over evolutionary time, it was in the reproductive interests of women and their families to grant men higher status, and for men and their families to limit women's status and control women's behavior, due to concerns with paternity certainty (Smuts 1995; Hopcroft 2002). This being said, there are some universal markers of individual status across human societies that are typically highly valued in mates, although there are important sex differences. There are also sources of social status that vary by the subsistence technology and level of complexity of the society. We review them here.

Age

In most human societies, people gain social status in their particular society as they age. There are no societies where children have a higher status than adults, for instance. Yet while greater age is universally associated with higher status and hence desirability as a mate for both men and women, there are sex differences in the effect of age on status and its association with desirability as

DOI: 10.4324/9781003463320-3

16   *Sources of social status across human societies*

a mate as we saw in Chapter 2. Given female preferences for status in a mate (and her family's preference that she marry a higher-status man), this means women prefer older partners, on average. Men (and their families) prefer younger partners, so in all societies we find women marrying men who are older than they are, on average. This means that on average fathers tend to be older than mothers. Using data from 130 countries and territories (home to 91% of the global population), Ausubel et al. (2022) found that men are an average of 4.2 years older than their wives or cohabiting partners. Wang et al.'s (2023) analysis of whole-genome data from the 26 populations in the 1000 Genomes Project show that over the past 250,000 years, fathers have been consistently older (average 30.7 years) than mothers (average 23.2 years). In contemporary societies this age gap varies across human societies depending on local conditions and cultures, and this was likely the case in the past. Wang et al.'s (2023) genomic data suggest that in the past most of this age gap is determined by changes in the age of paternity.

This does not mean that women are likely to prefer the oldest men, even though they are likely to have the highest status. Being older, any advantages their higher status offer their mates and children are offset by the fact that they are more likely to die in the near future than a younger man. Further, the genetic advantages older men offer their offspring are also limited, as advanced age in men is associated with a higher rate of de novo mutations in sperm (Kong et al. 2012). Correspondingly, children of older fathers have a higher risk for psychiatric morbidity (D'Onofrio et al. 2014), are slightly less attractive (Huber & Fieder 2014), and have a higher chance to remain unmarried and to have lower reproduction (Fieder & Huber 2015; Arslan et al. 2017).

Height and size for men

Particularly in polygynous social species of animals, males often fight for a higher rank, and a higher social rank is associated with a higher number of offspring. Elephant seals in the South Atlantic Ocean are a well-investigated example. Among elephant seals, fighting ability and dominance are associated with higher reproductive success in terms of copulation frequency (McCann 1981). In those species where ranking hierarchies among males depend on their ability to win competitions, rank is typically positively associated with body size, as larger and heavier individuals have a better chance of winning fights and dominance contests and monopolizing future matings. A meta-analysis of several studies on dominance and reproduction in primates showed that dominance is associated with various fitness aspects in a variety of species (Majolo et al. 2012). In most cases actual fights over dominance are avoided and rank is established by simply displaying the traits indicating fighting ability, although male contests do sometimes occur. Nonetheless, the sexual dimorphism (in primates larger males compared to females) in those species is rooted in the advantage larger body size provides

Sources of social status across human societies   17

in male–male competition, be it an actual fight or just the display of fighting ability (Fairbairn 1997).

Animal studies also show that body size is highly heritable. For instance, in polar bears (*Ursus maritimus*), body size has a heritability of 34%–48% (Malenfant et al. 2018). A comparable heritability estimate for morphological measures including body size of 25%–52% (depending on the exact measure) has been found for red deer (*Cervus elaphus*; Kruuk et al. 2002). Thus, in animal species body size is typically an indicator of social rank and is also highly heritable.

It is likely that similar processes of sexual selection have occurred among human males and is likely the most important cause of sexual dimorphism in body size in humans and the fact that men are on average larger and taller than women. Over evolutionary time, larger body size would have aided human males in conflicts with other men as well as other species. In 90% of the approximately 300,000 years or so of human existence when humans were hunting and gathering, greater height and larger body size would have been positively associated with both fighting and hunting ability. Greater height and associated longer legs would have been associated with faster running speed, which would be an asset in both hunting and battle. Upper body strength would generally have been an asset in fighting and in hunting as it would have been helpful in personal combat and throwing projectiles (rocks, spears, using bow and arrows) at game and enemies. Success at hunting and combat would likely have been associated with high social status, as is the case in historical cases that have been studied (see Chapter 4) and likely also associated with number of offspring.

Further, women who preferred larger, taller men with upper body strength who were good at hunting and combat and likely high in social status as a result were more likely to have their children and themselves well-nourished and protected. Women who preferred tall strong men who were good warriors and hunters as mates would also have received the benefits of kinship with a high-status man, and their children would also have received these benefits. Further, for women who prefer taller and larger men there will be a genetic advantage for their children, especially their male children, if they inherit genes for height and strength from their father. As in animals, in humans, body height is a highly heritable trait. Depending on sex and population, adaptive heritability of body height ranges from 68% to 93% with an average of about 80% (Silventoinen et al. 2003). Thus, there was likely selection for female preferences for males with larger body size.

While human females also compete for mates, there was unlikely similar selection processes for height in women. First, given greater maternal investment in offspring means a selective advantage for mothers that stay alive (Campbell 1999), so ensuring selection against tendencies toward violent combat and other risky activities in women, and little or no selection for characteristics useful in such activities such as height. As a result female mate competition is more likely to take the form of indirect competition

18　*Sources of social status across human societies*

rather than direct face-to-face combat. Given lesser advantages of height for women, there was also less likelihood of selection for male preferences for height in a mate.

There is evidence that larger men do tend to have higher social status and tend to be preferred as mates across all human societies (Mazur 2005). Even in most modern human societies where men are much less likely to earn status through hunting and combat, women still prefer tall, strong men, as mates (Jæeger 2011; Stulp & Barrett 2016). For example, in a large representative sample of men and women aged 15–77 from Canada, Cuba, Norway, and the U.S., Pisanski et al. (2022) found that women preferred taller than average men as mates, while men preferred shorter than average women as mates. Taller, stronger men are more likely to have children than other males (Pawlowski et al. 2000; Mueller & Mazur 2001). In modern societies, height is also positively associated with health and other measures of social status such as education and income (Meyer & Selmer 1999), which are also correlated with reproductive success. In women, however, evidence of selection on height is weak and if anything tends to favor shorter women (Nettle 2002).

Intelligence and costly signaling

While the association between body size, social status, reproduction, and selection may represent some analogy between animals and humans, the interdependence of body size and social status in humans is in fact much more complicated (reviewed in Stulp & Barrett 2016). For instance, successful strategies for attaining status beyond brutal force and dominance such as the friendship and alliance building found in many other species are also found in humans. Cognitive abilities are often the most important trait for gaining social status in humans, thereby decoupling body size and strength from social rank and reproductive success (Plomin 1999; Hill et al. 2019; Clark 2014). This is true for both men and women, as there is evidence that both men and women set a very high value on intelligence in their mates (Miller 2000; Prokosch et al. 2009). Individual cognitive abilities are revealed in a variety of ways that differ by society and cultural setting but include tactical skill in warfare and hunting, skill in cultural and intellectual activities, as well as political skill.

As in animals (see Chapter 2), there is also evidence of costly signaling to attain status in humans. A good example is the devotion to religion and the practice of costly rituals. Extreme cases are, for instance, the crucifixion on Good Friday at the Philippines, or the Hindu feast "Thaipusam," celebrated exhaustively in southern India and Malaysia, where men pierce needles through their skins and carry things on these needles. Other examples are the Ashura feast of Shia where Muslims flagellate themselves in public, or the celebration of the Semana Santa in Seville, where heavy frameworks with artwork of the saints are carried in processions through the city. All these rituals

Sources of social status across human societies 19

have in common that they are mostly performed by men. By showing their commitment to their own group they may rise in social status among their peers and gain in attractiveness as potential mating partners (Fieder & Huber 2012). It is not just participation in religious rituals that may be considered costly signaling. Throughout history, rulers and other elites have legitimized their rule (or aspirations to rule) with appeals to religion and investment in religious activities and institutions. In European history, for example, kings and others have endowed monasteries and churches with land and riches. They also undertook expensive and dangerous Crusades to the Holy Land.

An impressive example of the positive effect of costly signaling on social status and hence fertility is the extreme case of war heroism, which has been analyzed in U.S. soldiers who fought in World War II: Rusch et al. (2015) compared regular war veterans and those who have received the medal of honor, which is the highest U.S. war decoration for bravery and is usually awarded for saving someone's comrades at high personal risk. The results suggest that women find war heroes more sexually attractive than regular war veterans and associate war heroism with higher social status. As a result, war heroes had higher mating success and sired more children. Thus, the study provides evidence that war heroism conveys social status and that women may perceive war heroism as a costly signal of positive mate quality. Achievements in art, music, science, engineering, and other cultural areas to attain status and mates in human societies may also be interpreted within the costly signaling framework (Miller 2011).

Beauty (especially for women)

Beauty in humans is highly correlated with youth, health and fertility, all features attractive in mates for both men and women. Yet, as we have seen, men are more likely to prioritize youth, health, and fertility in a mate than women. Over the millennia that humans were hunting and gathering, the easiest way to ascertain that a potential mate was youthful, healthy, and fertile was to assess her appearance and hence her beauty, as the young and healthy tend to be more beautiful than the old and unhealthy. Men with genes that encouraged them to find beautiful mates were more likely to find young, healthy, and fertile mates and leave genetic descendants, so over evolutionary time there would have been selection for genes for these preferences. There would be less reproductive benefit for women who chose younger men as mates, and thus less selection for preferences for a beautiful mate. This means that women are less likely than men to prioritize a beautiful mate. The result is elevated status for beautiful women and elevated desirability as a mate, more so than for beautiful men.

There is evidence that beauty is prized across human societies and is a source of social status, particularly for women. Standards of beauty do vary by culture, but the correlates of youth and health – smooth, clear skin, white teeth, shiny hair, bright eyes, rosy lips and cheeks, comparatively fairer hair

20 *Sources of social status across human societies*

and lighter skin – are always associated with beauty, especially for women. There is evidence that beauty is associated with greater desirability in a mate. In the U.S., evidence suggests that facial beauty positively predicts marriage for both men and women, but more for women than for men (Jæeger 2011).

Sex, age, beauty, height and body size for men, intelligence, and costly signaling are sources of status in all societies, from the simplest through to the most complex. Throughout about 90% of human history that people lived as hunters and gatherers in foraging societies, there was little or no other basis for individual social rank besides these characteristics. People had few possessions, as hunters and gatherers are usually nomadic and carry their belongings from place to place. From studies of contemporary foraging societies, we can infer that in historical hunting and gathering societies political leadership was likely provided by a headman who would have had little power to enforce his will. Headmen in foraging groups usually have few privileges, although as befits their status they may have more than one wife. Hunting and gathering societies are typically highly egalitarian societies with status differences mostly based on sex, age, and individual abilities such as skill at hunting and warfare (Boehm & Boehm 2009).

Social status in agricultural societies

This is not true in societies beyond the hunting and gathering level of subsistence technology. With the beginning of agriculture, societies became more sedentary, larger, and the opportunity for larger economic and political differences between individuals and groups emerged. It is in simple horticultural or gardening societies that large political and economic differences between individuals and groups first develop. While it is difficult to know about social systems in historical horticultural societies, studies of recent horticultural societies in Melanesia, Polynesia, and the west coast of the U.S. show that the institution of a "big man" or similar high ranked man or chief is common. This is a person who, often with the aid of others who are politically connected to them, cultivates a large garden and accumulates valued objects, then holds a feast and gives away both foodstuffs and objects. Often there are multiple groups of individuals supporting different prospective big men, and the man or group who successfully holds the largest feast and gives away the most goods is awarded both authority and status within the group. The position of big man is subject to change, as any man and his supporters can successfully challenge the current big man by holding larger feasts and giving away more goods. Big men have more wives than other men, and as a result are likely to have more children. The institution of "big man" while found in many horticultural societies is not found in all. In some horticultural societies, such as the Yanomami discussed in Chapter 4, social status may simply be based on fighting ability. However, it is likely that at least in some horticultural societies in the past, institutions similar to the "big man" existed. In more complex horticultural societies, often permanent chiefs emerge, and are sometimes hereditary. These individuals and their relatives have the highest status in the group, and will often have rules of endogamy that prohibit marriage outside of the chiefly class. Such rules are a good way of helping to preserve a group's status. Even in chiefdoms there are usually few other social divisions, however. There is little occupational specialization in horticultural societies, although there are often people who occupy special religious positions. In some contemporary horticultural societies, these religious leaders can have a great deal of power and authority in the group, and the same was likely true in horticultural societies in history.

In horticultural societies, property rights in land are typically fluid. Horticulture is typically of the slash and burn type, where a field is slashed and burned and a crop is sown, then after a season or two depending on the fertility of the soil, the field is abandoned and a new field is created in a new location. In agrarian societies characterized by plow agriculture and less shifting cultivation, private property rights in land for individuals and groups become more defined, and the ownership of specific parcels of land clear. It is in these societies that ownership of land becomes a major source of social rank. Rights to land are also inherited, and in these societies, there usually emerges a political class that owns rights to most of the land, with a monarch or similar ruler at the top and an extensive aristocracy and group of lesser elites.

In foraging and horticultural tribal societies the subsistence base meant there was always an upper limit to the number of individuals in the group, albeit the exact number is somewhat in debate. This number is similar to the number of individuals who can possibly form a closely interacting group. According to the neo-cortex size of primates, Robin Dunbar estimated that "maximal group size" for human groups as not reasonably larger than 150 individuals (Dunbar 1993). This is a maximal group size that likely has been typical throughout our evolution. This is a group size where people know each other personally, group members are mostly kin, and where there is extensive social control against free-riders who try to exploit the group. In a group encompassing not more than 150 individuals, social hierarchies and associated inequality of social status and access to resources tend not to be very steep.

This all changed with the advent of intensive agricultural societies based on plow agriculture in the Levant, in the Fertile Crescent, as well as in East Asia. In these regions the first large settlements were founded. This process of the formation of larger settlements (the first cities and city-states) had a tremendous impact on the nature of social status as well as the inequality within societies (Scheidel 2017). As groups became larger, social hierarchies steepened and inequality became more pronounced. Ownership of property and access to resources became more important as indicators of social status than any other factor. This rise in inequality is impressively documented using the gini coefficient by Scheidel 2017. The Gini coefficient is a measurement of the inequality within a social group (it can be described not only in terms of income, but also in terms of other resources, even on the basis of calorie intake [Srivastava & Chand 2017]). A Gini coefficient of zero indicates perfect equality, whereas a Gini coefficient of one expresses maximal inequality – for instance, one person has all the income and all others have none. For tribal populations (hunter–gatherers and horticulturalists), the Gini coefficient was estimated as low as 0.25–0.27, for later herders it was estimated as 0.42, and for agriculturalists as 0.48 (reviewed in Scheidel 2017; Mulder et al. 2009).

Along with the increase of inequality and the steepening of social hierarchies in agrarian societies, the importance of intergenerational wealth transmission also increased (Scheidel 2017). Impressive examples of the increasing wealth and status inequality in more intensive agricultural societies can be found everywhere in the Near East, East Asia, the Americas, and as well as in Europe. An example lies in Middle Europe. From 800 until 450 before Christ, the so-called Hallstatt culture existed, named after the famous and picturesque village Hallstatt in the central Alps, where the "hall" – salt – had been mined and the prehistoric tunnels can still be visited. The Hallstatt culture was not restricted to the Alps but was found throughout Central and Western Europe and has been known later on as the "Celtic culture," which is well known as the culture of Asterix the Gaul. Its language still remains in parts of Great Britain and Ireland.

What is known to a lesser extent is that these earlier Celts not only established an impressive trade network with nearly every part of Europe, but also had large and powerful princely areas in the flat lands of middle Europe, presumably with several kingdoms and powerful kings. They built what is called in Austria the "Pyramids of Lower Austria" – burial mounds up to 15 meters high, in which the local king (or queen) has been buried with

Figure 3.1 "Pyramids" of lower Austria: burial mounds from the Hallstatt culture. Height presumably indicates social status of local "kings" and "queens" buried in the mounds. On the left, the highest burial mound (15 meters high "gross Mugl" [large mound]), on the right, a smaller one in a village close by. Picture by Martin Fieder and Susanne Huber.

Sources of social status across human societies 23

rich grave goods such as golden jewelry, pottery made of bronze, and highly decorated cult wagons (see Figure 3.1). We do not have written evidence, but these burial mounds may have indicated the social status of the king and his family by the height and scope, as there are many mounds of different sizes, and by the richness of the burial goods. As the Hallstatt culture in Austria may also have had large defensive castles and a differentiated craftsmanship, it is reasonable to assume that this society was also highly differentiated (Smrcka 2009; van der Vaart et al. 2017).

Sex differences in status also became pronounced in such large-scale agricultural societies. Part of the reason for this is that high-status men and their access to property and resources become disproportionately valuable as mates in such societies. As a result, high-status men and their families can be demanding about the personal characteristics of prospective mates, leading to greater control of women (particularly young women) in all aspects of their life, particularly control over their sexual behavior (Smuts 1995). Ideologies of female inferiority and male superiority help facilitate male control over women throughout such societies.

Sex and ownership of property are not the only basis for status in large-scale agricultural societies. In such complex societies there is usually a proliferation of occupations, all with different levels of social rank depending on the society. Individuals are typically grouped by family into occupational groupings, and there are typically rights, responsibilities, and rules attached to those groups. Some of the occupational groups provide service to a ruling class, such as a warrior class. There is always a highly ranked class of priests who not infrequently overlap with a scholarly class. Other occupational groups fulfil more everyday functions as farmers, potters, bakers, scribes, among many. Often occupations are inherited from father to son. While different occupational groupings have different statuses, there are typically strict rules concerning endogamy, so people who are in a certain group are obligated to marry others within the same group. Within endogamous groups, status is usually allocated by characteristics such as height, strength, property and income for men, and beauty for women. Sometimes the different occupational groupings become solidified into a full-blown caste system such as developed on the Indian subcontinent, with strict rules regarding endogamy and many other behaviors for each occupational caste.

The House of Habsburg – an example of status preservation

In agrarian societies, status is stably transmitted from one generation to the next, as has been impressively documented by the tracking of surnames (Clark 2014). The social status of certain groups and families can persist over centuries. An impressive example of how a group can attain status and preserve it over time by a clever "status policy" is given by the House of Habsburg in Austria. The Austrian Emperor Rudolf IV (November 1, 1339, to July, 27, 1365) was the most important figure of the Habsburg Empire

24   Sources of social status across human societies

for the following 600 years even though this period included several Holy Roman emperors such as Friedrich III, Charles V, Maria Theresa, and Joseph II. Charles V was the ruler of one of the largest empires of all times. His empire, including large parts of Europe and the Americas, was the so-called *empire where the sun never set.* Maria Theresa was the famous empress, who was among the first to make education compulsory for children (Berls 1970; Evans 1990). Her son, Joseph II, ruled in Austria at the time of Wolfgang Amadeus Mozart. After his regency, the Holy Roman Empire vanished (1806) and the Austro-Hungarian Empire emerged, lasting until the beginning of World War I. The last real ruling emperor of Austria was the popular Franz Joseph and his wife Sisi.

How could Rudolf IV gain such an enormous status and power for Austria and the Habsburg lineage? One simple reason is that he was clever, creative, and he did not cringe from fraud, maybe one of the most powerful and obvious frauds in history. The Viennese born Rudolf IV was Duke of Austria, Styria, and Carinthia from 1358 on. He was also Count of Tyrol, which is nowadays a small province of the small country Austria. Rudolf was a very energetic person, with a vision for his country and family. He aimed to gain independence from the Bishop of Passau (who was a powerful ruler in the Catholic Church) and wanted to be in charge of the Roman Catholic Church in Austria. As an impressive symbol, Rudolf started the Gothic expansion of the St. Stephen's Cathedral in Vienna, one of the most magnificent Gothic cathedrals in Europe (see Figure 3.2). In 1365 he also founded the University of Vienna, one of the oldest universities in Europe and meanwhile the oldest German-speaking university. With the "Wiener Pfennig," he further established a relatively stable currency.

His masterpiece, however, was an obvious fake which brought status and power to the Habsburgs for centuries: the so-called *Privilegium maius.* It was a forgery of documents that put the Habsburg dynasty to the level of the "Kurfürsten" (princeps elector imperii) of the Holy Roman Empire, which meant a tremendous and far-reaching increase in social status. The "Kurfürsten" have been the most powerful princes of the Holy Roman Empire. The name "Kurfürsten" relates to the fact that they elected among themselves the Emperor "Kaiser" (German from Julius Caesar) of the Sacrum Romanum Imperium in the tradition of Charles the Great, based on the medieval idea of a Christian Catholic successor of the ancient Roman emperors. Thus, due to the Privilegium maius, the Habsburgs got the status of an emperor of the Holy Roman Empire. It was a very cleverly made fake consisting of five documents based on older documents including the Privilegium minus from 1156. The Privilegium minus was a real document in which the legendary Holy Roman emperor Friedrich I, so-called Barbarossa (red beard), gave special rights to the House of Babenberger, the predecessor Austrian dynasty. Although even the contemporaries of Rudolf IV did recognize that the Privilegum maius was a forgery, for political reasons, it was finally confirmed 100 years later by the Habsburgian emperor Friedrich III.

Sources of social status across human societies 25

Figure 3.2 St. Stephen's Cathedral in Vienna. Picture by Martin Fieder and Susanne Huber.

26 *Sources of social status across human societies*

Without doubt, the very cleverly fabricated document was a cornerstone for the Habsburgian dynasty.

The Habsburgs are interesting also for another reason. Through the centuries, the Habsburg dynasty was not so much interested in warfare than in another, certainly evolutionarily important trade, namely "mating." In fact, most of the power the Habsburgs did gain over the centuries was achieved by a clever marriage politics, ensuring alliances and leading to many descendants and a European-wide "kin–network." The motto of the Habsburgs was *Bella gerant alii, tu felix Austria nube* (let the others fare wars, you lucky Austria marry).

Social status in industrial societies

The Industrial Revolution (usually dated to the late 18th century in Europe) marked a decisive break with the agrarian past. Employment in the new factories and mills increased while employment in agriculture decreased until in most industrial societies today it is less than 10% of the population. Populations became more urban than rural. The growth of industry and the development of complex economies meant increased standards of living for most people. Although inequalities remain, the primacy of family or group status and inheritance in determining individual status is much less than was typical in agrarian societies. The economic position and social status of individuals in industrial societies is determined mostly by individual factors, including education, individual occupation, individual and family income, ownership of property and other assets, although family background and the inheritance of status and wealth remain important. Individual political positions can also offer considerable individual status in industrial societies and usually also improve an individual's economic position. The nature of social status in industrial societies is further examined in Chapter 8.

To conclude, age, body size, intelligence, costly signaling, and beauty are likely sources of individual status across all societies at all levels of complexity and are associated with desirability as a mate. Sex itself is usually a source of social status, with males generally being granted somewhat higher status than females. Yet the historical emergence of plow agriculture and larger settlements of people was accompanied by greater social differentiation across sexes and social groups, greater material inequalities, as well as the greater inheritance of social status across generations. In these agrarian societies, both historically and in the contemporary world, group position in the social hierarchy and inheritance of status and resources is often the most important determinant of individual social status. While inheritance of wealth and status persists, in modern industrial societies these tendencies have become muted to some extent, and individual factors have again become important.

References

1000 Genomes Project, www.internationalgenome.org/1000-genomes-summary/ Last accessed November 15, 2023.

Arslan, R. C., Willführ, K. P., Frans, E. M., Verweij, K. J., Bürkner, P. C., Myrskylä, M., ... & Penke, L. (2017). Older fathers' children have lower evolutionary fitness across four centuries and in four populations. *Proceedings of the Royal Society B: Biological Sciences*, 284(1862), 20171562.

Ausubel, J., Kramer, S., Shi, A. F., & Hackett, C. (2022). Measuring age differences among different-sex couples: Across religions and 130 countries, men are older than their female partners. *Population Studies*, 76(3), 465–476.

Berls, J. W. (1970). *The elementary school reforms of Maria Theresa and Joseph II in Bohemia*. New York: Columbia University.

Boehm, C., & Boehm, C. (2009). *Hierarchy in the forest: The evolution of egalitarian behavior*. Cambridge, MA: Harvard University Press.

Campbell, A. (1999). Staying alive: Evolution, culture, and women's intrasexual aggression. *Behavioral and Brain Sciences*, 22(2), 203–214.

Clark, G. (2014). *The son also rises*. Princeton, NJ: Princeton University Press. ISBN-10: 0691168377.

Danner, J. E., Danner, R. M., Bonier, F., Martin, P. R., Small, T. W., & Moore, I. T. (2011). Female, but not male, tropical sparrows respond more strongly to the local song dialect: Implications for population divergence. *American Naturalist*, 178(1), 53–63.

D'Onofrio, B. D., Rickert, M. E., Frans, E., Kuja-Halkola, R., Almqvist, C., Sjölander, A., ... & Lichtenstein, P. (2014). Paternal age at childbearing and offspring psychiatric and academic morbidity. *JAMA Psychiatry*, 71:432–438.

Dunbar, R. I. (1993). Coevolution of neocortical size, group size and language in humans. *Behavioral and Brain Sciences*, 16(4), 681–694.

Evans, R. J. W. (1990). Maria Theresa and Hungary. In H. M. Scott (Ed.), *Enlightened absolutism: Reform and reformers in later eighteenth-century Europe* (pp. 189–207). Basingstoke: Macmillan.

Fairbairn, D. J. (1997). Allometry for sexual size dimorphism: Pattern and process in the coevolution of body size in males and females. *Annual Review of Ecology and Systematics*, 28(1), 659–687.

Fieder, M., & Huber, S. (2012). The association between pro-social attitude and reproductive success differs between men and women. *PLoS One*, 7(4), e33489.

Fieder, M., & Huber, S. (2015). Paternal age predicts offspring chances of marriage and reproduction. *American Journal of Human Biology*, 27(3), 339–343.

Hill, W. D., Davies, N. M., Ritchie, S. J., Skene, N. G., Bryois, J., Bell, S., ... & Deary, I. J. (2019). Genome-wide analysis identifies molecular systems and 149 genetic loci associated with income. *Nature Communications*, 10(1), 5741.

Hopcroft, Rosemary L. (2002). The evolution of sex discrimination, *Psychology, Evolution and Gender*, 4(1), 43–67.

Huber, S., & Fieder, M. (2014). Advanced paternal age is associated with lower facial attractiveness. *Evolution and Human Behavior*, 35(4), 298–301.

Jæger, M. M. (2011). "A thing of beauty is a joy forever"? Returns to physical attractiveness over the life course. *Social Forces*, 89(3), 983–1003.

28 Sources of social status across human societies

Kong, A., Frigge, M. L., Masson, G., Besenbacher, S., Sulem, P., Magnusson, G., ... & Stefansson, K. (2012). Rate of de novo mutations and the importance of father's age to disease risk. *Nature*, 488(7412), 471–475.

Kruuk, L. E., Slate, J., Pemberton, J. M., Brotherstone, S., Guinness, F., & Clutton-Brock, T. (2002). Antler size in red deer: Heritability and selection but no evolution. *Evolution*, 56(8), 1683–1695.

Majolo, B., Lehmann, J., de Bortoli Vizioli, A., & Schino, G. (2012). Fitness-related benefits of dominance in primates. *American Journal of Physical Anthropology*, 147(4), 652–660.

Malenfant, R. M., Davis, C. S., Richardson, E. S., Lunn, N. J., & Coltman, D. W. (2018). Heritability of body size in the polar bears of Western Hudson Bay. *Molecular Ecology Resources*, 18(4), 854–866.

Mazur A. (2005). *Biosociology of dominance and deference*. New York: Rowman & Littlefield.

McCann, T. S. (1981). Aggression and sexual activity of male southern elephant seals, *Mirounga leonina*. *Journal of Zoology*, 195(3), 295–310.

Meyer, H. E., & Selmer, R. (1999). Income, educational level and body height. *Annals of Human Biology*, 26(3), 219–227.

Miller, G. (2011). *The mating mind: How sexual choice shaped the evolution of human nature*. New York: Anchor.

Miller, G. F. (2000). Sexual selection for indicators of intelligence. In G. Bock, J. A. Goode, & K. Webb (Eds), *The nature of intelligence* (pp. 260–270). New York: Wiley (Novartis Foundation Symposium 233).

Mueller, U., & Mazur, A. (2001). Evidence of unconstrained directional selection for male tallness. *Behavioral Ecology and Sociobiology*, 50(4), 302–311.

Mulder, M. B., Bowles, S., Hertz, T., Bell, A., Beise, J., Clark, G., ... & Wiessner, P. (2009). Intergenerational wealth transmission and the dynamics of inequality in small-scale societies. *Science*, 326(5953), 682–688.

Nettle, D. (2002). Women's height, reproductive success and the evolution of sexual dimorphism in modern humans. *Proceedings of the Royal Society of London. Series B: Biological Sciences*, 269(1503), 1919–1923.

Pawlowski, B., Dunbar, R. I. M., & Lipowicz, A. (2000). Tall men have more reproductive success. *Nature*, 403, 156.

Pisanski, K., Fernandez-Alonso, M., Díaz-Simón, N., Oleszkiewicz, A., Sardinas, A., Pellegrino, R., ... & Feinberg, D. R. (2022). Assortative mate preferences for height across short-term and long-term relationship contexts in a cross-cultural sample. *Frontiers in Psychology*, 13, 937146.

Plomin, R. (1999). Genetics and general cognitive ability. *Nature*, 402(Suppl 6761), C25–C29.

Prokosch, M. D., Coss, R. G., Scheib, J. E., & Blozis, S. A. (2009). Intelligence and mate choice: Intelligent men are always appealing. *Evolution and Human Behavior*, 30(1), 11–20.

Rusch, H., Leunissen, J. M., & Van Vugt, M. (2015). Historical and experimental evidence of sexual selection for war heroism. *Evolution and Human Behavior*, 36(5), 367–373.

Scheidel, W. (2017). *The great leveler*. Princeton, NJ: Princeton University Press.

Silventoinen, K., Sammalisto, S., Perola, M., Boomsma, D. I., Cornes, B. K., Davis, C., ... & Kaprio, J. (2003). Heritability of adult body height: A comparative study of twin cohorts in eight countries. *Twin Research and Human Genetics*, 6(5), 399–408.

Smuts, B. (1995). The evolutionary origins of patriarchy. *Human Nature*, 6(1), 1–32.

Smrcka, V. (2009). Social evolution in the Hallstatt – La Tène period. *Acta Universitatis Carolinae Medica Monographia*, 156, 27–56.

Srivastava, S. K., & Chand, R. (2017). Tracking transition in calorie-intake among Indian Households. *Agricultural Economics Research Review*, 30(347–2017–2034), 23–35.

Stulp, G., & Barrett, L. (2016). Evolutionary perspectives on human height variation. *Biological Reviews*, 91(1), 206–234.

van der Vaart, S. A., Schumann, R., & van der Schumann, R. V. S. (2017). Differentiation and globalization in Early Iron Age Europe: Reintegrating the Early Hallstatt period (Ha C) into the debate. Connecting elites and regions: Perspectives on contacts, relations and differentiation during the Early Iron Age Hallstatt C period in Northwest and Central Europe.

Wang, R. J., Al-Saffar, S. I., Rogers, J., & Hahn, M. W. (2023). Human generation times across the past 250,000 years. *Science Advances*, 9(1), eabm7047.

4 Social status and fertility in preindustrial societies

In animal species, higher rank achieved by a great variety of means increases fitness and is to some extent comparable to the more complex concept of social status in humans. As we have seen in Chapter 3, in humans there are a variety of different sources of social status depending on the ecological, cultural, and historic context. However, in humans as in animal species there is likely to be a positive relationship between social status and reproductive success, particularly for men, as noted in Chapter 2. In this chapter we examine the evidence of this relationship for men and women in pre-industrial societies. Although historical and prehistorical evidence is often scarce, there is better evidence from contemporary preindustrial societies. We examine both where possible.

Hunting and gathering societies

What do we know about the relationship between social status and fertility in pre-historic hunting and gathering societies? From archeological records, we do not know very much. We therefore have to focus on those populations still living today and assume that prehistoric populations with similar subsistence technologies were somewhat similar. In these societies, the available data on male fertility show that high-status men in those societies out-reproduce low-status men. What constituted status for men can differ, but generally hunting ability earns status for men and is associated with a larger number of children. For example, among the hunting and gathering group the Aché of Paraguay, a man's hunting ability was positively correlated with his number of children (Kaplan & Hill 1985; Hill & Hurtado 1996). The same was true among the Meriam hunter–gatherers of Australia (Smith et al. 2003), the Hadza of Tanzania (Marlowe 2010), and among hunter–fisher trappers in northern Siberia (Ziker et al. 2016).

Among recently studied groups, the Hadza can be viewed as the typical forager society (Marlowe 2010). For the following portrayal, we refer to the intriguing book *The Hadza: Hunter-gatherers of Tanzania* (2010) by Frank M. Marlowe, who began his research in 1995 and has since visited the Hadza

DOI: 10.4324/9781003463320-4

Social status and fertility in preindustrial societies   31

15 times, spending a total of 4 years with them. With regard to complexity, together with the Mbuti Pygmies of the Democratic Republic of Congo, the Hadza are one of the least complex forager societies. They score 0 out of 40 on a measure of cultural complexity calculated by Murdoch and Provost (1973), which is based on parameters such as mode of subsistence, mobility, technological specification, social stratification, and several others. For comparison, most forager societies have a mean score of 6 on a scale ranging from 0 to 13.

The Hadza live in Northern Tanzania within an area of about 4,000 sq. km. There are roughly 1,000 Hadza, 300–400 of whom still live exclusively by hunting and gathering. Hadza are nonterritorial and move an average of 6.5 times per year between mobile camps of 2 to about 100 people with a mean camp size of 30. Camp residence is fluid, as people move in and out of camps, although each camp usually has a core group that tends to consist of a group of sisters. There is no higher social organization than the camp.

The Hadza is a very egalitarian society, where each individual has considerable autonomy. The reasons for egalitarianism in foragers such as the Hadza include that individuals do not have control over resources, do not have any material wealth, and the fact that due to their mobility they can easily escape bossy people. Hadza men are dominant over women and adults are dominant over younger individuals, but these inequalities are much smaller than in more complex societies. In addition, even though there are differences in hunting capability among men, and hunting reputation more than anything else creates at least a slight variation in status, it does not cause any dominance hierarchy.

There are also no clans in Hadza society. Descent is traced both through the mother and the father. Generally, bilateral descent is prevalent in foragers probably because it results in a higher number of kin across camps, increasing the likelihood for individuals to be welcomed in each camp. The murder rate is low, approximately the same as in the contemporary U.S. Nearly all murders are committed by men and caused by disputes over women. Warfare is rare and if it ever occurs, it is usually provoked by their pastoralist neighbors. Attacks among Hadza groups are extremely rare.

The Hadza exhibit a sexual division of labor. Men hunt large game, whereas women and children forage for plants such as tubers, berries, and baobab. As is the case in many forager societies, men usually hunt alone to get close enough to the prey. Only during the dry season do men hunt in pairs at night. Also typical for forager societies, food is widely shared among the members of the camp, particularly the food men bring into camp. About 57% of daily kcal is usually acquired by women. In married couples, however, about 50% of kcal, and if the wife is nursing, 69% of kcal are contributed by food brought in by men.

The Hadza mating system is serial monogamy in addition to a small amount of polygyny. Only about 4% of men are polygynous, but never with more than two wives, and these polygynous marriages tend not to be

32 Social status and fertility in preindustrial societies

stable. Nonetheless, variance in reproductive success is larger in men than in women. The main factor influencing Hadza marriage seems to be female choice. Women show a preference for good hunters. Accordingly, men with better hunting reputation have a higher reproductive success, mainly because they are married to younger wives and are more likely to remarry after the menopause of their previous wife. It is not quite clear why females show this preference for hunting ability in a mate because meat is shared widely outside the household. However, since a man's own children get a greater share of the food brought by men to camp, a woman does receive a benefit from her husband's provisioning. Also, if hunting ability is inherited, then the woman's sons and grandsons are more likely to be good hunters also.

Horticultural and tribal societies

In horticultural and tribal societies beyond the forager level of subsistence, there is evidence that for men status is positively associated with fertility, although the source of status varies. For the Yanomami of Venezuela, Chagnon (1988) presented evidence that having killed a man elevated a man's status and was associated with higher fertility. For the horticultural group the Yali of Papua New Guinea, the source of status for men was number of pigs owned (Sorokowski et al. 2013). Men with more pigs had more children, and they were also more likely to have multiple wives. Among the herding group, the Bakharwal of India, men with larger herd sizes had more children than other men (Casimir & Rao 1995). Among Caribbean farmers of Trinidad (Flinn 1986) and among the horticultural Kipsigis of Kenya (Borgerhoff Mulder 1987, 1988, 1990, 1995, 1996), it was land ownership that was positively correlated with number of children for men.

In these societies, more children means more kin, and more kin further serve the purposes of attaining greater status for individuals. The Yanomami are an illustrative example. They are a tribal population living in the rainforests of Venezuela and Brazil who have been extensively investigated for many years by Napoleon Chagnon. The Yanomami are at the transition from hunter gatherers to horticulturalists, and score 8 out of 40 on a measure of cultural complexity calculated by Murdoch and Provost (1973) compared to 0 out of 40 for the hunting and gathering Hadza. The Yanomami population consists nowadays of about 35,000 individuals living in up to 200 villages, mainly at the border of Venezuela and Brazil. Usually not more than 200 individuals live under a large common roof called the Shabono. The Yanomami are foraging horticulturalists; they grow bananas (mostly cooking plantains), gather fruit, and hunt for animals. Most of the Yanomami are monogamous, but some men practice polygyny. The Yanomami practice many rituals including feasts where neighbors are usually invited. Such an invitation, however, can be lethal in some cases as, for instance, when the Yanomami practice revenge for bloody events in the past. Thus, although invitation of a neighboring tribe usually has the function of building good contacts and alliances against other

Social status and fertility in preindustrial societies 33

tribes, sometimes it can end in the killing of the invited. That may be the case if there are some old debts, or if it is assumed opportune. This will happen even if relatives are living in the other tribe, which is not unusual. If a man wants to marry, he lives with the family of the presumptive bride (who is usually from another tribe) and works for the family as a "bridal suitor." After a year or so, the bridal suitor takes the wife to his own tribe.

The Yanomami do not have any noteworthy wealth. Hence, social status and rank are not determined on the basis of the resources an individual controls. Male social status, rank, and, as a result, access to females are defined by bravery and being fierce in combat. Combat usually means an ambush, where a group of men hide silently close to another tribe, and, when the time is right, moves into the village of the other tribe, killing some men and looting women. The chances of a man to marry or even marry more than one wife are increased if he has killed in combat and becomes Unokai, meaning "someone who has killed." Thus, having a wife or better yet, several wives is the primary indicator of social status among Yanomami men. It is rare for reproduction and the goal of social status to be so closely related to each other for men as in the case of the Yanomami. Wives not only mean social status, but they also mean reproductive success. Accordingly, most of the fights that break out within the tribe are caused by a quarrel over women (Chagnon 1988, 2013). This is also the case in the Hadza (see above), however, and may hold true for most societies (Betzig 1986), a fact that was already recognized by Darwin (Darwin 1871).

Among the Yanomami, high-status men who have access to more women usually also have more children. Two important facts are the result: their sons have more (half) brothers, who will cooperate in combat, and more (half) sisters, with whom they are able to build up a large marriage network (reciprocal marriage within patrilineages) and therefore future alliances, which is very important in this violent society. This strategy of cooperation between kin highlights one of the most important principles in evolution, the principle of inclusive fitness and the practice of kin selection, or the favoring of kin. As we saw in Chapter 2, according to the principle of inclusive fitness, individuals pass on their genes not only directly by their own children, but also by the offspring of their relatives. As a consequence, from an evolutionary perspective helping a relative is not altruistic but selfish, as it indirectly helps pass on your own genes to the next generation. The closer the percentage of shared genes with the relative the greater this effect will be. Yanomami cooperation relies heavily on cooperation between relatives and hence kin selection. For a man, kinship requires genuine paternity. It is thus not surprising that as in many other tribal and other cultures, female fidelity is of central importance, and is often violently controlled in Yanomami society.

For Yanomami men, the ultimate goal of reproduction coincides with social status in a way that they are both literally the same. This is, however, rather the exception than the rule. In many so-called despotic cultures, for instance, social status corresponds to the availability of resources according

34 *Social status and fertility in preindustrial societies*

to a position in a social hierarchy, and does not always enhance individual reproduction. But for Yanomami men, individual social status equals number of wives, children, and kin ties.

An impressive example of how Yanomami kin networks are associated with social status, access to women, and number of children is the "Shinbone clan," documented by Napoleon Chagnon. The patriarch of the clan Shinbone himself had 43 children with several women, his father had 14 children, 143 great children, and 401 great-great children, hence building an influential and powerful tribe glued by kinship. However, given the importance of kinship for cooperation, the more distantly related are kin, the weaker the "genetic glue." Thus, later in time, as documented by Napoleon Chagnon, fights, wars, and massacres among more distant kin were the rule not the exception.

The warlike Yanomami are very different to the more peaceful Hadza. Serial monogamy may be another reason why the Hadza society is much more untroubled than that of the polygynous Yanomami. Polygyny practiced by eminent men has always been a means of weaving large kin networks that in turn increase social status even further. On the downside, however, polygyny also makes a society more unstable and prone to violence. The sex ratio at birth is in humans about 50:50. Consequently, in a polygynous society some men must remain without a wife, and this often causes conflict. According to Henrich et al. (2012), even a quite small prevalence of polygyny will have dramatic effects on the mating chances of men. The current unrest in the Muslim world may be partly explained by the prevalence of polygyny (Fieder et al. 2018), leading to a large proportion of unmarried men in the Muslim world.

In tribal societies like the Yanomami, social status and the ability to win fights over resources and access to fertile women is determined by kinship – who has more kin has a higher chance to win fights (a simple application of Hamilton's rule). Also in the Tierra del Fuego, for example, any man who finds his relative and kin in a fight will come to help him. In addition, as in the case of the Yanomami, fights are determined by the "club law" (Chagnon 2013). The same holds true for the Copper Eskimos: men only commit a violent crime if they can be sure of being supported by kin and friends, and therefore do not fear revenge (Jenness 1922). In these societies, the main rule of law is coercion and force. The Maori of New Zealand, for instance, practiced "restitution by plunder" (Betzig 1986). Simple strength and kin networks determine the outcome. However, as the violent interactions and the asymmetries in those societies have increased, there has also been an increasing role of arbiters who help to solve troubles and have often been able to gain in social status and resources due to their function as such.

Female fertility

While in all these hunting and gathering, herding, fishing, and horticultural societies there is often a positive relationship between a man's status and his

Social status and fertility in preindustrial societies 35

reproductive success, there is a much weaker (albeit still positive) relationship for women. For example, in Papua New Guinea among the Yali tribe, the number of pigs was positively associated with both the number of children ever born and the number of living children, but the correlation was much larger for men than for women (the correlation between the number of pigs and number of living children was 0.42 for men and 0.27 for women; Sorokowski et al. 2013). Among farmers of the Caribbean, amount of land owned was associated with number of children for women as well as men, but the association was much stronger for men (Flinn 1986).

Given the sex differences in the relationship between status and number of children in tribal societies, it is not surprising that men can have higher average fertility and almost always a greater variance on fertility than women as expected from Bateman's principle. In Betzig's (2012) review, the means for fertility for men in tribal societies are given as ranging from a low of 3.6 children (for the Xavante of Brazil) to a high 12.42 children (among the Kipsigis of Kenya). For women, Betzig (2012) finds a low completed mean fertility of 3.6 children for the Xavante of Brazil and a high of 8.91 children among the Tsimane of Bolivia. Variances on completed fertility for women are also much lower than for men, and range from a low of 3.57 for the Aché to a high of 12.69 among the Tsimane of Bolivia. For men variances on completed fertility range from a low of 8.07 for the Yomut of Iran to a high of 39.64 among the Yanomami of Venezuela (Betzig 2012).

Agrarian and despotic societies

The higher inequality and steeper hierarchies in agrarian societies mean huge differences in social status among individuals, and it is particularly men on top of the social ladder who benefit reproductively. These men of high social status are able to increase their number of progeny in ways unseen before in simpler societies. The reason is that they are now able to offer huge amounts of resources to their wives and progeny. Even though polygyny has ever been present in the history of *Homo sapiens*, during the emergence of larger states or "despotic societies" as Laura Betzig called them (Betzig 1986), it reached unprecedented dimensions.

Most human cultures have been polygynous to some degree. The actual number differs depending on the culture examined, but a rough estimate is that about 80% of all cultures (both in the past and in the present) are polygynous and correspondingly 20% are monogamous or strictly monogamous. However, in polygynous societies typically only a small fraction of men actually practice polygyny. In these societies, most of the men are either engaged in monogamous relationships or do not have any relationship at all (reviewed in Scheidel 2008). This is a pattern that we also see in contemporary industrial societies: men of low social status have a disproportionately high chance of remaining unmarried and childless (see Chapter 8), whereas men of high social status often practice some sort of serial monogamy, which

36 Social status and fertility in preindustrial societies

is in fact a form of hidden, legal polygyny (De la Croix & Mariani 2015; Fieder & Huber 2023).

In polygynous societies, a nontrivial fraction of men will not find a spouse. As a result, polygynous societies are likely to be engaged in warfare more frequently and to be more violent in general. This has two consequences: (1) conflict and war lead to casualties among men, which reduce the skewed marital sex ratio, and (2) the winners may obtain access to the women of the defeated (reviewed in Scheidel 2008). This view is supported by the fact that archeologists very rarely find young fertile women among victims of violence. Instead, most of the victims are men, male children, and the elderly (reviewed in Schahbasi et al. 2021).

From the female perspective, evolutionary theory predicts that under certain economic conditions it would make sense for a woman to join a polygynous union. In terms of own resources and resources available for the offspring, it could be more beneficial to be in a polygynous relationship, even as the secondary or even higher-order wife, of a man holding many resources than to be the only wife of a poorer man (Altmann et al. 1977). Yet observational results suggest a more complex association (Mulder 1989), with clear benefits only found for first wives in polygynous marriages compared to wives in monogamous relationships or higher-order wives in polygynous relationships (Gibson & Mace 2007).

The evolution of early large-scale societies and their stabilization by often drastic rules (e.g., code of Hammurabi) and also by new religions with so-called big gods (see also Sheehan et al. 2022), assured the accumulation of wealth over generations for a small ruling class, leading to extremely high inequality and to tremendous reproductive benefits for male rulers. A few powerful men obtained access to many young and fertile women. They were *despots who used their power to reproduce*. The extent of polygyny varied with population size. In small societies, men of high status may only have had a handful of wives, up to ten or so. In larger societies, the number of wives may have increased to hundreds. In some large-scale societies despotic "god-kings" may have had several thousands of wives and countless offspring. The African empire of Dahomey in West Africa at the Bay of Benin is representative of this development. In the 19th century the royal harem consisted of thousands of wives who had been recruited by the king among war captives. As a result, most of the inhabitants of the empire were in some way related to the king.

In despotic societies, for men position in the social hierarchy is thus strongly correlated with reproduction – the higher in the social hierarchy a man is, the more wives and children he has (Betzig 1986, reviewed in Scheidel 2008). Another example is the Inca Empire. At an age between 8 and 10, large numbers of girls were taken from their birth places to live in so-called Houses of the Chosen Women. These girls were divided into several categories according to their origin, attractiveness, and abilities. Out of these women in the "houses," the most beautiful ones were selected as the secondary wives of

Social status and fertility in preindustrial societies 37

the Inca king (de la Vega and Livermore 2010, pp. 297–301; Rostworowski de Diez Canseco 1999, pp. 176; Scheidel 2008). Again, the cultural success of the Inca king was associated with tremendous reproductive success, maximizing the genetic contribution to the next generation.

Despite this extensive progeny of the Inca king, resources and status were still limited to only a privileged minority: only the progeny of the king with his first order wife "the queen" (often his sister, for as in many despotic monarchies marriage between the Inca king and his sister was not only permitted but also favored) were considered noble and legitimate successors in line with the social status of the "divine father." Children of concubines who were themselves related to the king also had some special privileges. The children of the king from nonrelated women, however, did not inherit any privileges but retained the status of their mothers (Garcilasco de la Vega 1871, pp. 297–301; reviewed in Betzig 1986). Comparable customs have been found in other societies with concubinage (Scheidel 2008). Systems where inbreeding is associated with social status are not uncommon because (moderate) inbreeding has often been used, and is still used, to keep material wealth within families (Thornhill 1991). As is often the case, the despotic system of the Inca reign was justified in part by religion, mainly the "cult of the sun."

With the development of large-scale settlements, we find these despotic, highly unequal societies with often draconian rules, big gods (see Chapter 9), and previously unknown reproductive advantages for the leading men due to their often almost unlimited access to fertile women and extreme forms of polygyny. Despite such systems of concubinage, in several of these societies monogamy was officially the rule. This held true, for instance, for the Sumerian and Babylonian societies in the Fertile Crescent. It certainly also held true for ancient Rome. Despite living in an officially monogamous society, the son of Emperor Marcus Aurelius, Commodus, has been said to have had about 300 wives.

All these systems of concubinage have in common that despots' children born by concubines (the bastards) only inherited their mother's social status, leading to social oblivion (to some extent comparable to the Inca). In societies like ancient Rome, however, bastards contributed to the reproductive success of their father. Many of the concubines in Rome were slaves. Slaves could free themselves at a price. But many masters also freed their illegitimate children. Even though those children could not inherit their father's social status, when they were freed they often increased in social status, which in turn increased their chances of reproduction. In addition, illegitimate sons often got positions associated with some social status that had been arranged by their fathers, thereby increasing their own and hence also their father's reproductive success over generations.

An impressive example how far a "bastard" may come is William the Conqueror "the bastard" (1028–1087) from the Norsemen genus of the Rollides (after the founder Rollo 860–930, famously portrayed in the

38 Social status and fertility in preindustrial societies

U.S.–Canadian television series "Vikings"). William the Conqueror was the ruler of Normandy. He was the son of Robert I and Herleva, a second wife of Robert I. This union was without the blessing of the church, which is why it was said that William was a "bastard." Nonetheless, he conquered Anglo-Saxon England in 1066 by victory at the Battle of Hastings, and established a ruling class whose descendants live on (as evidenced by the disproportion of people with Anglo-French names among the English elite demonstrated by Clark (2014, p. 83)).

There are other striking examples on the tremendous fitness advantage that despotic systems offered the men in charge: Patricia Balaresque et al. (2015) showed on the basis of data from the Y chromosome that millions of Asians living today are descended from just eleven men who were alive between 2100 BC and AD1600, including several "Khans" of the Mongols and likely including Genghis Khan. Genghis Khan himself had so many children that he managed to spread his Y chromosome to about 1 in 200 of all men alive today (Callaway 2015). Despotism did pay off in terms of fitness. We can imagine that, albeit on a smaller scale, the Celtic elites who built the "pyramids of middle Europe" (see Chapter 3) likely still contribute to the genetic makeup of people in contemporary Middle Europe. Archeogenetics now has the means to find evidence for that claim.

While rulers of agrarian societies had tremendous reproductive success, the positive relationship between status and number of children for men was pervasive in agrarian societies at all levels of society. For example, in pre-industrial Western Europe, marriage for men was dependent on the acquisition of land, wealth, and/or an occupation. According to Petersen (1960), this was expressed in the preindustrial Netherlands as the principle 'that a man might not marry until his living was assured', and this idea that men could not marry until they could afford to support a family was widespread across preindustrial Europe (Habakkuk 1953). Men with no access to resources (low-status men) by and large did not get married and typically did not have children. Further, those men with more land or wealth had more children than other men. For example, among Krummhörn farmers in Germany during the 18th and 19th centuries, men with more land had more children and more descendants than other men (Voland 1988, 1990; Voland & Dunbar 1995). Among men in Lancashire, England, in the 18th century, those who owned land had the highest fertility (Hughes 1986). Clark (2007) used probate data to determine male fertility for 17th-century England and found that wealthier men had more children. In non-Western agrarian societies there is also evidence that higher-status males have more offspring. In pre-modern China, rich men married early and repeatedly, while poor men married later or not at all (Feng et al. 2010). In much of both historical and contemporary sub-Saharan Africa and parts of Asia, the custom of bride price ensures that only men with means can afford to get married, and only very wealthy men can afford to have more than one wife. For a comprehensive list of studies

Social status and fertility in preindustrial societies 39

showing a positive relationship between status and reproductive success for men, see Table 4.1.

Status and fertility among women in agrarian societies

Studies of female fertility in agrarian societies give mixed results, such that in several cases fertility differences between women of different classes are minimal and higher-status women do not always have higher fertility (Dribe et al. 2014, p. 173). Some studies do show higher fertility among elite women, but the differences between women of different classes are much smaller than for men. For example, Bengtsson and Dribe (2014) examined the general marital fertility rates (births to married women divided by the person years at risk for married women 15–49 years) for women aged 15–49 for data from 1815 to 1939 in Scania (in modern-day Sweden). At this time Scania was a farming region that had not yet experienced the fertility decline characteristic of the demographic transition (see Chapter 5). They found that women in the upper class (measured by the occupation of the family head, i.e., husband) had higher fertility in 1815–1829 (prior to the demographic transition). Differences by status were not great, with a marital fertility rate of about 400 children per thousand women per year for the elites and about 250 children per thousand women per year for the lower classes. Vézina et al. (2014) examined data on the fertility of women in pre-transition Quebec. They focused on the reproductive history of all women in first marriages, measuring a woman's status as her husband's occupational status. They found that before the demographic transition began, the wives of higher-status, nonmanual workers had the highest numbers of births, although differences between occupational groups were very small. The average number of births per family was 10 children for the nonmanual class and 8.5 children for the lower/unskilled class. Evidence from pre-transitional Asia also suggests that high-status women had higher fertility than low-status women (Tsuya et al. 2010). In northeastern China between 1789 and 1840, wives of well-off husbands were more likely to have later births, as revealed by household registries (Feng et al. 2010). Studies from preindustrial farming villages in central and eastern Japan found that landholding was positively associated with the fertility of married women (Tsuya & Kurosu 2010).

For these women in pre-demographic transition societies their fertility often did not reach Hutterite levels (about 12 children per woman over the course of her lifetime) and there was much variation from society to society. For example, in pre-transition Netherlands, the general marital fertility rate in the Netherlands was about 350 per thousand per year (Bras 2014), while in pre-transition Scania in Sweden, the general marital fertility rate was only 250 children per thousand women per year (Bengtsson & Dribe 2014). In pre-transition Quebec, the mean number of total births to women in first marriages was about eight (Vézina et al. 2014).

Table 4.1 Studies showing a positive relationship between male status and number of surviving offspring

Society	Status measure	Reference(s)
Aché of Paraguay	Hunting ability	Kaplan & Hill 1985; Hill & Hurtado 1996
Aka-Mormons	Political status	Walker & Hewlett 1990
Aka of the Central African Republic	Political status	Hewlett 1988; Walker & Hewlett 1990
Bakkarwal of India	Prestige, wealth	Casmir & Rao 1995
Caribbean farmers	Land ownership	Flinn 1986
Dogon of Mali	Land ownership, income	Strassman 1997
Efe of Zaire	Wealth	Bailey 1991
Finnish population, 18th and 19th centuries	Land ownership	Courtiol et al. 2012
Gabbra of Kenya	Wealth	Mace 1996a, 1996b
Medieval Europeans	Wealth, power	Betzig 1992, 1993, 1995
Modern Hungarians	Education	Bereczkei & Csanaky 1996
Ifaluk	Wealth	Turke & Betzig 1985; Betzig 1988
Kipsigis of Kenya	Land ownership	Borgerhof Mulder 1987, 1988, 1990, 1995, 1996
Krummhörn farmers of the 18th and 19th centuries	Land ownership	Voland 1988, 1990; Voland & Dunbar 1995
!Kung of the Kalahari	Social status	Pennington & Harpending 1993
Lancashire farmers of the 18th century	Occupational status	Hughes 1986
Mormons of Utah	Wealth, religious rank	Faux & Miller 1984; Mealey 1985
Mukogodu of Kenya	Wealth, social status	Cronk 1991
Norwegian farmers of the 18th to 20th centuries	Age, wealth	Røskaft et al. 1992
Portuguese elites of the 16th to 18th centuries	Land ownership	Boone 1986
Qing China	Rank in nobility	Lee & Campbell 1997; Lee et al. 1993; Wang et al. 1995
Ancient Romans	Wealth, power	Betzig 1992
Modern Swedes	Occupational status	Forsberg & Tullberg 1995
Swedish farmers of the 19th century	Occupational status, land ownership	Low 1991; Low & Clark 1992
Yali of Papua New Guinea	Number of pigs	Sorokowski et al. 2013
Yanomami	Political status	Chagnon 1979, 1980, 1988
Yomut Turkmen of Iran	Wealth	Irons 1979, 1980

Source: Compiled by Hopcroft.

Social status and fertility in preindustrial societies   41

These studies typically rely on measuring the fertility of married women in households, so omitting any consideration of the fertility of women who did not marry. These unmarried women were disproportionately elite women. For example, in 17th-century France, it was mostly the daughters of upper class families that populated nunneries and hence almost always had no children (Jones & Rapley 2001). In Florence, in the 17th century, about 44% of the daughters of aristocratic families were placed in convents before marriage age (Litchfield 1969). Among the Portuguese elite in preindustrial Europe, about 35% of elite women were sent to monasteries (Boone 1986). In China and India, the reproductive success of elite women was limited by the practice of female infanticide, non-remarriage of widows, and widow suicide for elite women (Dickemann 1979). This persisted into the early 20th century in India, where upper-caste women were frequently not allowed to remarry after the death of a spouse (Banerjee 1999). In 18th- and 19th-century India, two elite clans – the Jhareja Rajuts and the Bedi Sikhs – went so far as to kill all their daughters at birth, thus effectively bringing female fertility in these high-status clans to zero. Lower-status groups killed only later-born daughters (Hrdy 2000). In Japan, widow remarriage was uncommon among elites, and elite women often entered nunneries (Dickemann 1979).

In sum, there is ample evidence that for men in preindustrial societies, status was positively related to reproductive success for men, even though absolute levels of fertility and the sources of social status differed across historical, cultural, and economic settings. The positive relationship between status and fertility for men reached its apogee in despotic agrarian societies, where the highest status men could have hundreds of children. For women there is also evidence of a positive relationship between status and fertility, but it is much smaller than for men and sometimes nonexistent.

References

Altmann, S. A., Wagner, S. S., & Lenington, S. (1977). Two models for the evolution of polygyny. *Behavioral Ecology and Sociobiology*, 2, 397–410.

Bailey, R. (1991). *The behavioral ecology of Efe Pygmy men in the Ituri Forest*, Zaire. Ann Arbor University of Michigan Museum of Anthropology.

Balaresque, P., Poulet, N., Cussat-Blanc, S., Gerard, P., Quintana-Murci, L., Heyer, E., & Jobling, M. A. (2015). Y-chromosome descent clusters and male differential reproductive success: Young lineage expansions dominate Asian pastoral nomadic populations. *European Journal of Human Genetics*, 23(10), 1413

Banerjee, K. (1999). Gender stratification and the contemporary marriage market in India. *Journal of Family Issues* 20(5), 648–676. –1422.

Bengtsson, T. & Dribe, M. (2014). The historical fertility transition at the micro level: Southern Sweden 1815–1939. *Demographic Research*, 30, 493.

Bereczkei, T., & Csanaky, A. (1996). Mate choice, marital success, and reproduction in a modern society. *Ethology and Sociobiology*, 17, 17–36.

Betzig, L. (1986). *Despotism and differential reproduction: A Darwinian view of history*. Hawthorne, NY: Aldine.

42 Social status and fertility in preindustrial societies

Betzig, L. (1988). Mating and parenting in Darwinian perspective. In L. Betzig, M. Borgerhoff Mulder, & P. Turke (Eds), *Human reproductive behaviour: A Darwinian perspective* (pp. 3–20). Cambridge (UK): Cambridge University Press.

Betzig, L. (1992). Roman polygyny. *Ethology and Sociobiology*, 13, 309–349.

Betzig, L. (1993). Sex, succession and stratification in the first six civilizations: How powerful men reproduced, passed power on to their sons, and used power to defend their wealth, women and children. In L. Ellis (Ed.), *Social stratification and socio-economic inequality*, (Vol. 1, pp. 37–74). New York: Praeger.

Betzig, L. (1995). Medieval monogamy. *Journal of Family History*, 20, 181–215.

Betzig, L. (2012). Means, variances, and ranges in reproductive success: Comparative evidence. *Evolution and Human Behavior*, 33(4), 309–317

Boone, J. L. (1986). Parental investment and elite family structure in preindustrial states: A case study of late medieval–early modern Portuguese genealogies. *American Anthropologist*, 88, 859–878.

Borgerhoff Mulder, M. (1987) Cultural and reproductive success: Kipsigis evidence. *American Anthropologist* 89, 617–634.

Borgerhoff Mulder, M. (1988) Reproductive success in three Kipsigis cohorts. In Clutton-Brock, T. H. (Ed.) *Reproductive Success: Studies of Individual Variation in Contrasting Breeding Systems*. University of Chicago Press.

Borgerhoff Mulder, M. (1989). Marital status and reproductive performance in Kipsigis women: Re-evaluating the polygyny-fertility hypothesis. *Population Studies*, 43(2), 285–304.

Borgerhoff Mulder, M. (1990) Kipsigis women's preferences for wealthy men: evidence for female choice in mammals? *Behavioral Ecology and Sociobiology* 27, 255–264.

Borgerhoff Mulder, M. (1995) Bridewealth and its correlates. Quantifying changes over time. *Current Anthropology* 36, 573–603.

Borgerhoff Mulder, M. (1996) Responses to environmental novelty: changes in men's marriage strategies in a rural Kenyan community. In Maynard Smith, J. (Ed.) *Evolution of Social Behavior Patterns in Primates and Man*. British Academy Press, London.

Bras, H. (2014). Structural and diffusion effects in the Dutch fertility transition, 1870–1940. *Demographic Research*, 30, 151–186.

Callaway, E. (2015). Genghis Khan's genetic legacy has competition. *Nature News*.

Casimir, M. J., & Rao, A. (1995). Prestige, possessions and progeny: Cultural goals and reproductive success among the Bakkarwal. *Human Nature*, 6, 241–272.

Chagnon, N. A. (1979). Is reproductive success equal in egalitarian societies? In N. A. Chagnon, & W. Irons (Eds.), *Evolutionary biology and human social behavior: An anthropological perspective* (pp. 374–401). North Scituate, MA7 Duxbury Press.

Chagnon, N. A. (1980). Kin selection theory, kinship, marriage and fitness among the Yanomamö Indians. In G. Barlow, & I. Silverberg (Eds.), *Sociobiology: Beyond nature/nurture?* (pp. 545–71). Boulder, CO: Westview Press.

Chagnon, N. A. (1988). Life histories, blood revenge, and warfare in a tribal population. *Science*, 239(4843), 985–992.

Chagnon, N. A. (2013). *Noble savages: My life among two dangerous tribes – the Yanomamo and the anthropologists*. New York: Simon & Schuster.

Clark, G. (2007). *A farewell to alms: A brief economic history of the world*. Princeton University Press.

Clark, G. (2014). *The son also rises*. Princeton, NJ: Princeton University Press.

Courtiol, A., Pettay, J. E., Jokela, M., Rotkirch, A., & Lummaa, V. (2012). Natural and sexual selection in a monogamous historical human population. *Proceedings of the National Academy of Sciences*, 109(21), 8044–8049.

Cronk, L. (1991). Wealth, status and reproductive success among the Mukogodo of Kenya. *American Anthropologist*, 93, 345–360.

Darwin C. (1871). *The descent of man, and selection in relation to sex*. Princeton, NJ: Princeton University Press. ISBN-10: 1522766146.

De la Croix, D., & Mariani, F. (2015). From polygyny to serial monogamy: A unified theory of marriage institutions. *Review of Economic Studies*, 82(2), 565–607.

De la Vega, G. and Livermore, H.V. (2010). *Royal commentaries of the Incas*. pp. 297–301. Piki. Available, at google books: https://www.google.com/books/edition/The_Royal_Commentaries_of_the_Incas_and/ic4IBAAAQBAJ?hl=en&gbpv=1&dq=royal+commentaries+of+the+inca&printsec=frontcover

Dickemann, M. (1979). The ecology of mating systems in hypergynous dowry societies. *Social Science Information*, 18, 163.

Dribe, M., Oris, M., & Pozzi, L. (2014). Socioeconomic status and fertility before, during, and after the demographic transition: An introduction. *Demographic Research*, 31, 161.

Faux, S. F., & Miller, H. (1984). Evolutionary speculations on the oligarchic development of Mormon polygyny. *Ethology and Sociobiology*, 5, 15–31.

Feng, W., Campbell, C., & Lee, J. Z. (2010). Agency, hierarchies, and reproduction in northeastern China 1789 to 1840. In N. O. Tsuya et al. (Eds), *Prudence and pressure: Reproduction and human agency in Europe and Asia, 1700–1900* (pp. 287–316). Cambridge, MA: MIT Press.

Fieder, M., & Huber, S. (2023). Increasing income pressure on US men to find a spouse. *Biodemography and Social Biology*, 1–19.

Fieder, M., Huber, S., Pichl, E., Wallner, B., & Seidler, H. (2018). Marriage gap in Christians and Muslims. *Journal of Biosocial Science*, 50(2), 145–160.

Flinn, M. (1986). Correlates of reproductive success in a Caribbean village. *Human Ecology*, 14, 225–243.

Forsberg, A. J. L., & Tullberg, B. S. (1995). The relationship between cumulative number of cohabiting partners and number of children for men and women in modern Sweden. *Ethology and Sociobiology*, 16, 221–232.

Gibson, M. A., & Mace, R. (2007). Polygyny, reproductive success and child health in rural Ethiopia: Why marry a married man? *Journal of Biosocial Science*, 39(2), 287–300.

Habakkuk, H. J. (1953) English population in the eighteenth century. *Economic History Review* 6(2), 117–133.

Henrich, J., Boyd, R., & Richerson, P. J. (2012). The puzzle of monogamous marriage. *Philosophical Transactions of the Royal Society London B*, 367, 657–669.

Hill, K., & Hurtado, A. M. (1996). *Ache life history*. New York: Aldine de Gruyter.

44 *Social status and fertility in preindustrial societies*

Hrdy, S. B. (2000) *Mother Nature: Maternal instincts and how they shape the human species.* New York: Ballantine Books.

Hughes, A. L. (1986) Reproductive success and occupational class in eighteenth-century Lancashire, England. *Social Biology* 33(1–2), 109–115.

Irons, W. (1979). Cultural and biological success. In N. A. Chagnon, & W. Irons (Eds.), *Evolutionary biology and human social behavior: An anthropological perspective* (pp. 257–272). North Scituate, MA7 Duxbury Press.

Irons, W. (1980). Is Yomut social behavior adaptive? In G. W. Barlow, & J. Silverberg (Eds.), *Sociobiology:Beyond nature/nurture?* (pp. 417–473). Boulder, CO7 Westview Press.

Jenness, D. (1922). *The life of the Copper Eskimos.* Ottawa: F. A. Acland.

Jones, M. B., & Rapley, E. (2001). Behavioral contagion and the rise of convent education in France. *Journal of Interdisciplinary History*, 31(4), 489–521.

Kaplan, H. & Hill, K. (1985) Hunting ability and reproductive success among male Aché foragers. *Current Anthropology* 26, 131–133.

Kaplan, H., Gurven, M., Hill, K., & Hurtado, A. M. (2005). The natural history of human food sharing and cooperation: A review and a new multi-individual approach to the negotiation of norms. In H. Gintis et al. (Eds), *Moral sentiments and material interests: On the foundations of cooperation in economic life* (pp. 75–113). Cambridge: MIT Press.

Kruuk, L. E., Clutton-Brock, T. H., Slate, J., Pemberton, J. M., Brotherstone, S., & Guinness, F. E. (2002). Heritability of fitness in a wild mammal population. *Proceedings of the National Academy of Sciences*, 97(2), 698–703.

Lee, J., & Campbell, C. (1997). *Fate and fortune in rural China: Social organization and population behavior in Liaoning* (pp. 1774–1873). Cambridge, UK: Cambridge University Press.

Lee, J., Campbell, C., & Wang, F. (1993). *The last emperors: An introduction to the demography of the Qing imperial lineage.* In D. Rehler, & R. Schofield (Eds.), New and old methods in historical demography (pp. 361–382). Oxford, UK7 Oxford University Press.

Litchfield, R. B. (1969). Demographic characteristics of Florentine patrician families, sixteenth to nineteenth centuries. *Journal of Economic History*, 29(02), 191–205.

Low, B. S. (1991). Occupational status, land ownership, and reproductive behavior in 19th century Sweden: Tuna Parish. *American Anthropologist*, 92, 115–126.

Low, B. S., & Clark, A. L. (1992). Resources and the life course: Patterns through the demographic transition. *Ethology and Sociobiology*, 13, 463–494.

Mace, R. (1996a). When to have another baby: A dynamic model of reproductive decision-making and evidence from the Gabbra pastoralists. *Ethology and Sociobiology*, 17, 263–273.

Mace, R. (1996b). Biased parental investment and reproductive success in Gabbra pastoralists. *Behavioral Ecology and Sociobiology*, 38, 75–81.

Mealey, L. (1985). The relationship between social and biological success: A case study of the Mormon religious hierarchy. *Ethology and Sociobiology*, 6, 249–257.

Murdoch, G. P., & Provost, C. (1973). Factors in the division of labor by sex: A cross-cultural analysis. *Ethnology*, 12(2), 203–225.

Pennington, R., & Harpending, H. (1993). *The structure of an African pastoralist community: Demography, history and ecology of the Ngamiland Herero.* New York: Oxford University Press.

Social status and fertility in preindustrial societies 45

Petersen, W. (1960). The demographic transition in the Netherlands. *American Sociological Review*, 25, 334–347.

Røskaft, E., Wara, A., & Viken, Å. (1992). Reproductive success in relation to resource-access and parental age in a small Norwegian farming parish during the period 1700–1900. *Ethology and Sociobiology*, 13(5–6), 443–461.

Rostworowski de Diez Canseco, M. (1989). Ordenanzas para el servicio de los tambos de repartimiento de Huamachuco hecho por el licenciado Gonzalez de Cuenca, Revista Historica 36, Lima.

Schahbasi, A., Huber, S., & Fieder, M. (2021). Factors affecting attitudes toward migrants – an evolutionary approach. *American Journal of Human Biology*, 33(1), e23435.

Sheehan, O., Watts, J., Gray, R. D., Bulbulia, J., Claessens, S., Ringen, E. J., & Atkinson, Q. D. (2022). Coevolution of religious and political authority in Austronesian societies. *Nature Human Behaviour*, 1–8.

Scheidel, W. (June 2008). Monogamy and polygyny in Greece, Rome, and world history. Online working paper at: https://citeseerx.ist.psu.edu/document?repid=rep1&type=pdf&doi=c10d6d3623d3db8604d865f80b37c2a5bc94f97e

Smith, E. A., Bird, R. B. & Bird, D. W. (2003) The benefits of costly signaling: Meriam turtle hunters. *Behavioral Ecology* 14(1), 116–126.

Sorokowski, P., Sorokowska, A., & Danel, D. P. (2013). Why pigs are important in Papua? Wealth, height and reproductive success among the Yali tribe of West Papua. *Economics & Human Biology*, 11(3), 382–390.

Strassman, B. (1997). Polygyny is a risk factor for child mortality among the Dogon. *Current Anthropology*, 38, 688–695.

Thornhill, N. W. (1991). An evolutionary analysis of rules regulating human inbreeding and marriage. *Behavioral and Brain Sciences*, 14(2), 247–261.

Tsuya, N. O., Feng, W., Alter, G., Lee, J. Z., et al. (2010). *Prudence and pressure: Reproduction and human agency in Europe and Asia, 1700–1900*. Cambridge, MA: MIT Press.

Tsuya, N. O., & Kurosu, S. (2010). Family, household, and reproduction in northeastern Japan, 1716 to 1870. In N. O. Tsuya et al. (Eds), *Prudence and pressure: Reproduction and human agency in Europe and Asia, 1700–1900* (pp. 249–286). Cambridge, MA: MIT Press.

Turke, P., & Betzig, L. (1985). Those who can do: Wealth, status and reproductive success on Ifaluk. *Ethology and Sociobiology*, 6, 79–87.

Vézina, H., Gauvreau, D., & Gagnon, A. (2014). Socioeconomic fertility differentials in a late transition setting: A micro-level analysis of the Saguenay region in Quebec. *Demographic Research*, 30, 1097–1128.

Voland, E. (1988) Differential infant and child mortality in evolutionary perspective: data from the late 17th to 19th century Ostfriesland (Germany). In Betzig, L. et al. (eds) *Human Reproductive Behavior*. Cambridge University Press, pp. 253–276.

Voland, E. (1990). Differential reproductive success within the Krummhörn population (Germany, 18th and 19th centuries). *Behavioral Ecology and Sociobiology*, 26(1), 65–72.

Voland, E., & Dunbar, R. I. M. (1995). Resource competition and reproduction: The relationship between economic and parental strategies in the Krummhörn population (1720–1874). *Human Nature*, 6, 33–49.

46 *Social status and fertility in preindustrial societies*

Walker, P. L., & Hewlett, B. S. (1990). Dental health diet and social status among Central African foragers and farmers. *American Anthropologist*, 92, 383–398.

Wang, F., Lee, J., & Campbell, C. (1995). Marital fertility control among the Qing nobility: Implications for two types of preventative checks. *Population Studies*, 49, 383–400.

Ziker, J. P., Nolin, D. A. & Rasmussen, J. (2016) The effects of wealth on male reproduction among monogamous hunter–fisher–trappers in northern Siberia. *Current Anthropology* 57(2), 221–229.

5 Status and fertility in Europe and America during the demographic transition

As we have seen, the positive relationship between status and fertility predicted by evolutionary theory has appeared in all preindustrial societies, from the simplest to the most complex. Social elites, in particular, elite men (although not always elite women), had more children than others and more of those children survived to have children themselves. But as societies began to develop and industrialize in the late 18th century, a major demographic change began that resulted in fertility rates declining to unprecedentedly low levels. This change is called the demographic transition and it occurred first in the societies that developed and industrialized first – the societies of north-western Europe, and some of their former colonies – but as the countries of East Asia industrialized in the second half of the 20th century, it occurred there too. This chapter describes the relationship between status and fertility for women, and where possible, for men, during the demographic transition in Europe and America.

The demographic transition

The demographic transition generally refers to the four stages of demographic change that all modern industrial societies have gone through as they industrialized and developed. The first stage is the stage of high mortality and high fertility typical of the agricultural societies that existed in Europe and Asia prior to the Industrial Revolution. In such societies death rates are high, particularly child mortality rates, and a child is lucky to live to its first birthday. If a child does live to its first birthday, it still has a substantial chance of dying from one of the many infectious diseases that people suffer in premodern societies, including cholera, typhoid fever, diphtheria, scarlet fever, typhus, gastrointestinal diseases, polio, and tuberculosis. The spread of these diseases is assisted by the crowding of people in cities and the lack of public health facilities such as sewerage systems and clean water supplies. These infectious diseases infected Europeans and to a somewhat lesser extent Americans in large numbers throughout the 19th century, as they do in most agrarian societies.

DOI: 10.4324/9781003463320-5

48   *Status and fertility in transitioning Europe and America*

In northwestern Europe, mortality rates probably first began to decline in the mid-17th century. The reasons were several. First there was an improvement in agricultural production and the production of more food, meat in particular, that helped keep people better nourished, healthier, and more able to resist infectious diseases. Second, governments and other authorities increasingly built public works, such as sewerage systems and other infrastructure, to keep sewerage out of water supplies and provide a cleaner supply of drinking water. Other public works included the draining of marshes and swamps, which removed breeding grounds for mosquitos and other insects that spread disease. There were also organized efforts to control the number of rodents, particularly in cities, and this also helped stop the spread of disease.

Third, there were improved practices at the household level (Mokyr 1993). The import of cheap cotton cloth from India in the 18th and 19th centuries led to the increased use of cotton clothing that was washed and changed more frequently than the woolen clothes of the past and less likely to harbor disease-carrying fleas and lice. Soap also became more widely used on a daily basis, for washing both clothes and people, and its antibacterial effects were helpful in preventing infection. The development of indoor toilets linked to sewerage systems and their widespread use by the 19th century also helped control diseases such as cholera. By the 19th century generally increasing affluence and the rise of a middle class who could afford to live in less crowded and dirty conditions helped slow the spread of disease, particularly in urban regions. Improved ways of preserving food, including canning and later the introduction of pasteurization, at first for wine and later for milk, also lowered rates of infectious disease.

The resulting decline of infectious diseases particularly improved infant mortality, and infants became more likely to see their first birthday. This did much to improve life expectancy at birth, which rose from below 40 in most of 18th-century Europe to over 50 by the beginning of the 20th century (Coale 1984). In the middle of the 20th century, improved medical technology, especially the development of antibiotics and improved methods of immunization, as well as the chemical control of disease carriers led to a further decline of deaths from infectious disease. For example, after the first sulfa antibiotics were introduced in the U.S. in 1937, mortality rates from pneumonia (a leading cause of child mortality) declined by 17%–32% (Bhalotra et al. 2018). In England and the U.S., life expectancy at birth had reached 70 years of age by 1970.

For the first century or so after the beginning of the decline in mortality rates in Europe, fertility rates stayed high. This period of low mortality and continuing high fertility is referred to as the second stage of the demographic transition. The mismatch between high pre–transition fertility together with decreased mortality always results in a rapidly growing population. From an evolutionary perspective, it is not surprising that there is a lag between the fall in child mortality and the fall in fertility. The memory of high mortality

Status and fertility in transitioning Europe and America 49

and its perceived threat may keep birth rates high, as families continue to have high fertility in order to replace those who might die. To have many children in such an environment, where mortality is perceived as being high even if it has been starting to decrease, may be the remnant of an evolved adaptive strategy (Mace 2000; Hill & Kaplan 1999) to have "spare" children in a high mortality environment.

This period of growing population did not last in Europe. At varying times and at varying speeds, fertility rates began to decline all over Europe and the third stage of the demographic transition began. France was one of the first European countries to see a decline in fertility, with the decline dating to about 1827 (Coale & Treadway 1986). Other countries of Northern and Western Europe followed at later dates, with the decline in many countries beginning around the year 1900. Countries in Southern and Eastern Europe lagged behind, with declines not starting until about 1920. Generally the earlier the decline began, the slower it went. In all regions of Europe, from start to finish, the overall decline in fertility was about 50% in the average number of children born to a woman (Coale & Treadway 1986).

At first the primary way the fertility decline occurred in Europe was through a rising age at marriage that limited the number of children a couple could possibly have. By the beginning of the 20th century, in about half the provinces of Europe, married couples were also starting to limit the number of children they had, regardless of age at marriage. In some parts of Europe fertility was already at replacement level by 1900. For example, Coale and Treadway (1986, p. 34) note that in 1900, three provinces in Europe already had replacement fertility levels. They were Lot-et-Garonne (a *departement* of France), Geneva (Switzerland), and County Tipperary in Ireland, where total fertility rates (TFRs – the number that can be thought of as the number of children the average woman will likely have in her lifetime) were about 2.1, 2.0, and 2.7 children per woman, respectively. Fertility decline continued throughout Europe until after World War II, when fertility rates rose briefly during the post-war baby boom. In 1960 TFRs throughout the provinces of Europe were about 2.48 (Coale & Treadway 1986, p. 62). After 1960, TFRs fell again to below replacement in almost all European countries (Coale & Treadway 1986, p. 78).

In the U.S. fertility rates were higher than they were in Europe, but the decline in fertility also began in the 19th century. The TFR was a little under 3.5 births per woman in 1911 and then fell to replacement levels of just over 2 during the Great Depression. After World War II, the baby boom saw a rise in TFR to about 3.6 in 1961, falling again to below replacement during the energy crisis of the 1970s (Population Reference Bureau 2012). These declining rates of fertility in Europe and America (and in the former colonies of each) have continued, with some interruptions, until the present. The resulting pattern of low mortality rates and low fertility rates is referred to as the fourth or final stage of the demographic transition.

50 *Status and fertility in transitioning Europe and America*

Status and fertility during the demographic transition

Most of the study of the fall of fertility rates associated with the third stage of the demographic transition is based on aggregate data concerning countries and regions, not individual data with information about individuals' personal status and number of offspring (Dribe et al. 2014a). When individual data are available, it is usually data on the fertility of women in households. As noted in Chapter 1, evolutionary theory suggests a somewhat different relationship between status and fertility for males and females, so both male and female fertility should be examined. Yet male fertility has been very little studied in the completed demographic transitions of Europe and America, so it is difficult to examine male and female fertility separately.

For women, studies show that women in middle class families (the wives of professionals, managers, and clerical and sales personnel) were typically the first to limit fertility, while the wives of farmers and unskilled workers were the last to do so (Livi-Bacci 1986; Dribe et al. 2017). For example, Dribe et al. (2014b) look at the relationship between status and fertility in five societies at an early stage of the demographic transition – Canada, Iceland, Sweden, Norway, and the U.S. – using census data from 1900. They examine recent net fertility or the number of own children aged less than 5 years living in the household of currently married women aged 15–54. The woman's status was measured by the occupational status of her husband. They find that low fertility in all these transitional societies was characteristic of the wives of professional and nonmanual men, while farmers' wives had the highest fertility of all.

Another study in America shows it was the wives of white-collar workers who were first to change their fertility behavior. Maloney et al. (2014) examined women's fertility by differences in husband's occupations for women in Utah born from the 1850s to the 1910s, a period at the beginning of the fertility transition in this region. Data came from the Utah Population Database, a database that includes information on the residents of Utah from the mid-1800s to the mid-1970s. Husbands' occupations (and any occupations ever held by wives) were found from death certificates. Only women who were born in Utah, had survived at least to age 50, had married once, who remained married to that spouse, and who had at least one child were included in the analysis. They find that women in farm families had the highest fertility at the beginning of the period, but other than that differences between occupational groups in number of children ever born were small. The mean number of children for women born in the 1850s in Utah in the very early stages of their transition was 8.95 children per woman. The wives of farmers had a mean number of children of a little over nine children, the wives of white-collar workers had a mean of a little over eight children. For all women, age at marriage rose for all the birth cohorts until 1870, and once again the wives of men in white-collar occupations led the way in that trend. This trend toward rising age at marriage ended with the 1870 birth cohort.

Status and fertility in transitioning Europe and America 51

After the 1890s birth cohort the wives of men in all occupational groups increasingly delayed childbearing after marriage and this was responsible for most of the fertility decline after this point. For the women born in 1910, the wives of white-collar workers had a mean number of children of a little under 4, the wives of farmers had a mean number of children of about 4.5 children.

Little is known about male fertility in Europe or America, as most studies examine female fertility only. Studies such as those just described that focus on female fertility or the number of children in the household omit the males who never marry and never form a household. These men tended to be the poorest men and those without any occupation at all, as there was a strong link between male access to resources and marriage all over preindustrial Europe (Petersen 1960), and the same was true in preindustrial America. This custom persisted through the 19th century when fertility began to fall. Not all women married, but there was no legal or normative link between possession of resources and marriage for women as there was for men. In Europe rural women often worked before marriage, mostly as servants in the towns, but this usually ended when they married (Fauve-Chamoux 1998). Thus studies that find a negative relationship between male status (as measured by white-collar occupation) and fertility based on female fertility alone will likely overestimate the negative relationship between male status and fertility in the early stages of fertility decline.

In Europe as fertility declined over the course of the 20th century, fertility levels between wives of men in all occupational groups converged, with the exception of farmers and unskilled workers who tended to lag behind. Even in 1935–1968 Scania (Sweden), families headed by farmers and low-skill workers had about a 30% greater chance of higher-order births than managers, professionals, people in clerical and sales positions, and skilled workers (Dribe et al. 2017). The U.S. followed a similar trajectory. A study of U.S. Census data using only white women 20–69 years of age, who had been married once and were living with their husbands, found that the wives of professionals, proprietors, and clerks had the lowest fertility, while farm owners and laborers continued to have the highest fertility from 1910 to 1940 (Dinkel 1952), a pattern that continued in the U.S. to 1952 (Westoff 1954). By 1970 the wives of farm laborers and farm foremen, and to a lesser extent farm owners and managers, continued to have the highest fertility, but fertility differentials between women by this time were slight (U.S. Census 1973).

A consistent trend in both Europe and America over the course of the demographic transition was the inverse relationship between fertility and years of education for women (Westoff 1954; Skirbekk 2008), a trend that continues to this day (see Chapter 8). There are a variety of reasons for this trend. On a genetic level, data from modern Western populations show that the association between genes for education and completed fertility is negative for both women and to a lesser extent men, hence, the same genomic sequences associated with higher education are also associated with reduced

52 *Status and fertility in transitioning Europe and America*

fertility (Beauchamp 2016; Kong et al. 2017; Fieder & Huber 2022; see Chapter 8). Thus, those who have a higher genetic predisposition for education may also have a lower genetic predisposition for fertility. Although these findings are from modern populations in Europe and America, these negative genetic associations between education and fertility likely also existed in the past. Yet, in modern populations these genetic associations only explain a very small proportion of the negative association between fertility and education, as by far most of the negative association between education and fertility is explained by factors such as a delay in marriage and the postponing of first birth, and the same was likely true in the past also.

Women who were employed outside of the home also had lower fertility than women not working for pay (Moore et al. 2021). For example, Dribe et al. (2014b) found using census data from Canada, Iceland, Sweden, Norway, and the U.S. in 1900 that after controlling for a variety of individual characteristics, women in the labor force had much lower fertility than other women. In fact they found the effect of female employment on fertility was greater than most of the effects of socioeconomic class. Moore et al. (2021) used data on women under 40 from parishes in Scotland between 1851 and 1901 and found that women in employment had fewer children than those not in employment. Maloney et al. (2014) found that up until the 1870s birth cohort in Utah, only about 4% of women had an occupation reported for any point in their life. This rose to about 29% among the 1910 birth cohort. For all women, having an occupation at any point in their lives was generally associated with a lower number of children ever born. As with other fertility differences by status, these differences between women of different education levels and employment status have narrowed in recent years.

Income is another important measure of social status, usually correlated with education and occupation but imperfectly so. Most studies using income as a measure of individual status use family income, not individual income. In a large study of class differences in fertility using primary and secondary sources from the 1870s to the 1940s (a period that covers most of the period of the demographic transition) for Great Britain, the U.S., Norway, Sweden, France, Australia,Germany, Switzerland, Denmark, and Canada, Wrong (1958) finds three trends in the relationship between family income and fertility. The most common pattern was that family income and number of children were negatively associated for everyone except the highest income families, who had somewhat higher fertility so the relationship had a reverse J shape. He notes that this pattern was found among public-service employees in 1906 in France; among numerous cities in the U.S. in the 1930s and in the 1940s; in Melbourne, Australia, in 1942; in urban Sweden in 1936; and in Canada in 1941. Sometimes this trend was amplified to the extent that the relationship between family income and fertility became U-shaped, with the lowest income and the highest income families having the largest number of children and the middle income groups having the fewest number of children. More rarely still the trend was actually a positive relationship

Status and fertility in transitioning Europe and America   53

with higher-income families having the largest number of children. Wrong speculated that this pattern suggested that the inverse relationship between status and fertility characteristic of the third stage of the demographic transition may in fact tend to change over time from a reverse J-shaped curve to a U-shaped pattern, and may eventually lead to a positive relationship – a prescient prediction as we will see in Chapter 7.

We have seen in this chapter how in Europe and America it was educated women and the wives of men in nonmanual occupations who were the first to lower their fertility. Evidence on male fertility is much less abundant than evidence on female fertility, but it also mostly suggests there was a negative relationship between status (as measured by education, occupational status, and family income) and fertility for men also. This pattern is echoed in East Asia, as we see in Chapter 6.

References

Beauchamp, J. P. (2016). Genetic evidence for natural selection in humans in the contemporary United States. *Proceedings of the National Academy of Sciences*, 113(28), 7774–7779.

Bhalotra, S. R., Venkataramani, A. S., and Walther, S. (2018). Fertility and labor market responses to reductions in mortality, ISER Working Paper Series, No. 2018–15, University of Essex, Institute for Social and Economic Research (ISER), Colchester.

Coale, A. J. (1984). The demographic transition. *Pakistan Development Review*, 531–552.

Coale, A. J. and Treadwell R. (1986). A summary of the changing distribution of overall fertility, marital fertility, and the proportion married in the provinces of Europe. In A. J. Coale & S. C. Watkins (Eds), *The decline of fertility in Europe* (pp. 31–181). Princeton, NJ: Princeton University Press.

Dinkel, R. M. (1952). Occupation and fertility in the United States. *American Sociological Review*, 17(2), 178–183.

Dribe, M., Breschi, M., Gagnon, A., Gauvreau, D., Hanson, H. A., Maloney, T. N. & Vézina, H. (2017). Socio-economic status and fertility decline: Insights from historical transitions in Europe and North America. *Population Studies*, 71(1), 3–21.

Dribe, M., Oris, M. & Pozzi, L. (2014a). Socioeconomic status and fertility before, during, and after the demographic transition: an introduction. *Demographic Research* 31, 161.

Dribe, M., Hacker, D. J. & Scalone, F. (2014b). The impact of socioeconomic status on net fertility during the historical fertility decline: A comparative analysis of Canada, Iceland, Sweden, Norway and the U.S.A. *Population Studies* 68(2), 135–149.

Fauve-Chamoux, A. (1998). Servants in preindustrial Europe: Gender differences. *Historical Social Research/Historische Sozialforschung*, 112–129.

Fieder, M., & Huber, S. (2022). Contemporary selection pressures in modern societies? Which factors best explain variance in human reproduction and mating? *Evolution and Human Behavior*, 43(1), 16–25.

Kong, A., Frigge, M. L., Thorleifsson, G., Stefansson, H., Young, A. I., Zink, F., ... & Stefansson, K. (2017). Selection against variants in the genome associated with

54 Status and fertility in transitioning Europe and America

educational attainment. *Proceedings of the National Academy of Sciences*, 114(5), E727–E732.

Livi-Bacci, M. (1986). Social-group forerunners of fertility control in Europe. In A. J. Coale & S. C. Watkins (Eds), *The decline of fertility in Europe: The revised proceedings of a conference on the Princeton European Fertility Project* (pp. 182–200). Princeton, NJ: Princeton University Press.

Mace, R. (2000). Evolutionary ecology of human life history. *Animal behaviour*, 59(1), 1–10.

Maloney, T. N., Hanson, H. & Smith, K. (2014) Occupation and fertility on the frontier: evidence from the state of Utah. *Demographic Research* 30, 853–886.

Mokyr, J. (1993). Technological progress and the decline of European mortality. *American Economic Review*, 83(2), 324–330.

Moore, F., Lumb, E., Starkey, C., McIntosh, J., Benjamin, J., Macleod, M., & Krams, I. (2021). Women's trade-offs between fertility and employment during industrialisation. *Humans*, 1(2), 47–56.

Petersen, W. (1960). The demographic transition in the Netherlands. *American Sociological Review*, 25, 334–347.

Population Reference Bureau 2012. www.prb.org/resources/the-decline-in-u-s-fertility/ Last accessed November 17, 2023.

Skirbekk, V. (2008). Fertility trends by social status. *Demographic Research*, 18(5), 145–180.

U.S. Census (1973). 1970 Census of Population, supplementary report: Age at first marriage and children ever born, for the United States: 1970, April 1973 Report Number PC(S1)-34. www.census.gov/library/publications/1973/dec/population-pc-s1-34.html Last accessed November 17, 2023.

Westoff, C. F. (1954). Differential fertility in the United States: 1900 to 1952. *American Sociological Review*, 19(5), 549–561.

Wrong, D. H. (1958). Trends in class fertility in Western nations. *Canadian Journal of Economics and Political Science/Revue canadienne de economiques et science politique*, 24(2), 216–229.

6 Status and fertility in East Asia during the demographic transition

Although Europe, America, and other countries of European origin were the first to complete all stages of the demographic transition, since World War II, the industrialization and development of much of East Asia – including Japan, Taiwan, South Korea, and China – has been accompanied by a complete (and rapid) demographic transition. Once again the timing and pace of the change has been different in each country, but now all have low (often below replacement) fertility (Atoh et al. 2004). East Asia in fact now leads the world in levels of childlessness (Sobotka 2021). For the world as a whole the transition to very low fertility rates has been particularly consequential in China, as it has long been the most populous country in the world.

The demographic transition occurred with hitherto unseen speed in East Asia. For example, the decline in mortality and increase in life expectancy characteristic of stage two took a 100 years in France, where life expectancy increased from 40 to 70 between 1800 and 1900 (Davis 1963). This same process took only about 50 years in China. The fertility decline from six to three children per women characteristic of stage three took more than 100 years in European countries (e.g., the U.K. or Poland, see Skirbekk 2022), whereas it took only 20 years or even less in Korea, Bangladesh, China, and Iran (Roser et al. 2014). The main reason for the discrepancy between East Asia and European countries is that in East Asia as in contemporary transitioning societies, mortality rates have decreased much faster than they did in European countries, in part due to the import of effective public health practices and modern medical technology.

Japan

Japan was the first non-European or society not of European origin to experience the demographic transition. Mortality began to fall in about 1870, largely in response to the modernization of Japan by the new government after the Meiji Restoration of 1868. The Meiji government actively promoted industrial enterprises such as iron foundries, shipyards, and model factories. They also built a national railroad system, improved harbor facilities, built public

DOI: 10.4324/9781003463320-6

56 Status and fertility in East Asia

utility services such as water, electricity, and gas, and set up a public education system. Land reform transferred much land from the former Tokugawa ruling class to farmers, and this helped promote subsequent growth in agricultural productivity. Domestic savings from the agricultural economy helped provide investment for the further development of secondary industry (manufacturing and construction) as well as the finance, transportation, public utilities, government, trade, and service industries in Japan. From 1878 to 1938, real incomes in Japan rose thirteen-fold (Bronfenbrenner 1961).

The Meiji government also introduced the *koseki* law, or Family Registration System Law, by which every person in Japan had to be registered and counted. The first population data released by this system occurred in 1872. After 1920, the *koseki* law was replaced by a census of the population every 5 years. Due to these systems, there are reliable data on Japanese demography after 1870. These data show that the crude death rate fell from about 27 per thousand in 1870 to about 17 per thousand in 1940. Life expectancy at birth improved from 32 years of age for men and 35 years of age for women in 1870 to 47 for men and 50 for women in 1940 (Atoh 2008, p. 6). As in Europe, most of the decline in mortality came from declines in infant and child mortality due to the fall in infectious disease, with the exception of deaths from tuberculosis, which may have risen at this time. The decline in infectious disease was largely due to improvements in nutrition, personal health and hygiene, and public health. Some of these improvements were due to state effort, such as public works and the introduction of universal primary school education, and some were due to the rising affluence afforded by increasing incomes.

Fertility in Japan rose between 1870 and 1920, likely because of improvements in the population registration system that better enumerated births as well as better nutrition and the banning of abortion in 1880 (Atoh 2008). Fertility did not begin to decline until about 1920. Between 1925 and 1940, fertility declined from a total fertility rate (TFR) of about 5.1 births per woman to 4.1. After a post-war spike in the fertility rates, fertility began to fall again until it reached replacement level in about 1957 (Atoh et al. 2004; Atoh 2008). This rapid fertility decline accompanied the equally rapid industrialization and economic growth of Japan after World War II. The Gross National Product (GNP) of Japan grew at a rate of 9% annually from 1955 to 1960. By 1970, Japan had become the third largest economy in the world in terms of GNP, after the U.S. and the Soviet Union (O'Bryan 2009, p. 4).

Most of the decline in fertility between 1920 and 1940 was due to the postponement of marriage (Atoh et al. 2004), but the decline of fertility within marriage also played a role. Like other countries, after World War II, Japan experienced a baby boom due to a temporary increase in marital fertility. This petered out rapidly, and since the 1950s most of the fertility decline has been due to the postponement of marriage and the decline of the proportion married. For example, among women aged 45–49, the percentage of unmarried rose from 1.9% in 1960 to 6.3% in 2000 (Jones 2005). The

Status and fertility in East Asia   57

postponement of marriage has been particularly notable in Japan in recent years (Atoh et al. 2004; Raymo et al. 2015). For example, the percentage of young women aged 25–29 who were never married grew from 18% in 1975 to 60% in 2010 (Piotrowski et al. 2015). Associated with the postponement of marriage and the decline in the proportion married is the rise in childlessness. The proportion of Japanese women who are childless increased from 11.6% of those born between 1943 and 1948 to 27.6% for those born between 1971 and 1975 (Ghaznavi et al. 2022). Of women born in 1972, 28% were permanently childless, one of the highest rates in the developed world (Sobotka 2021). There has also been an increase in childlessness within married couples in Japan. For women born from the late 1920s to 1950s, childlessness among married women was about 3%–4%. Since the 1960s, childlessness among married women has increased so that 10% of married women born between 1965 and 1970 are permanently childless (Sobotka 2021).

As in Europe and America, it is more educated women who led the way in Japan's fertility decline after World War II. Between 1955 and 1975 the high school enrollment rate of the high-school-aged population increased from 56% to 91% for males and 47% to 93% for females. The college enrollment rate of the college-aged population increased from 15% to 44% for males and 5% to 33% for females (Atoh 2008). In Japan, women with more education are more likely to marry late or never marry, and the expansion of educational opportunities for women thus played a role in the decline of fertility to below replacement fertility. In Japan (as in most Asian countries) there are very few births outside of marriage, so unmarried women are very unlikely to ever have children. In contemporary Asia only 2%–4% of births take place outside of marriage, compared, for example, to 60% in France (Sobotka 2021). For women the negative relationship between education and fertility increased during the 1980s and early 1990s but has decreased recently (Raymo et al. 2015). For example, Ghaznavi et al. (2022) find that the fertility difference between those with university education and those without a university education widened for the cohorts born between 1956 and 1970, but for the 1971–1975 birth cohort the difference between more educated and less educated women has become negligible and not significant.

As for historical Europe, for Japan there is less information on male fertility than female fertility. However, there is evidence of a negative relationship between education and fertility for men as well as for women, although it is smaller for men than women and with the most recent cohorts of men appears to be reversing. Shirahase (2000) in a study of women born between 1925 and 1975 found that the wives of men in white-collar professional or managerial positions were less likely to have a first child than the wives of men in unskilled manual positions (Shirahase 2000). Yet Ghaznavi et al. (2022) find that men with a university degree had more children across all birth cohorts except the oldest one (1943–1947) although the differences were only statistically significant among those born between 1956 and 1960.

58   *Status and fertility in East Asia*

The reason for this change is that men with a higher level of education are more likely to be married than men with a lower level of education (Atoh et al. 2004; Piotrowski et al. 2015). This trend has increased in recent years. Between 1960 and 2000, the proportion of men aged 45–49 who were unmarried in Japan increased from 1.4% to 14.6% (compared to from 1.9% to 6.3% for women; Jones 2005), and these unmarried men were disproportionately men with low levels of education. In contemporary Japan less educated men are less likely to have a secure, full-time job or a high income, and it is men who have a full-time, standard employment and high income who are most likely to be married and have children (Piotrowski et al. 2015; Tsuya 2023). For example, data from Tokyo and Aomori in 2003 show that among 25- to 34-year-old men, full-time workers were most likely to be married, while part-time workers were most likely to have never married. In 2003 in Aomori 70% of 25- to 34-year-old men in the lowest income category were unmarried, compared to only 15% of men in the highest income category. In Tokyo 85% of 25- to 34-year-old men in the lowest income category were unmarried, while only 35% respectively of men in the highest income category remained unmarried (Ogawa et al. 2009, Table 3.3). Men with high incomes also have more children. Ghaznavi et al. (2022) found a positive relationship between annual income and number of children for Japanese men from all birth cohorts from 1943 to 1975. This positive relationship between income and fertility for men in post-demographic transition societies is also seen in Western societies (see Chapter 7).

Taiwan

As in Japan, the demographic transition in Taiwan proceeded quickly. From 1910 to 1930 there had been something of an agricultural revolution in Taiwan, particularly in the sugar and rice industries with Japanese investment while Taiwan (then known as Formosa) was a colony of Japan. This became an important economic basis for the industrialization of Taiwan after World War II, guided by the Taiwanese government and facilitated by U.S. aid and investments from mainland China and the overseas Chinese. Foreign trade took off after 1960, with Taiwan producing agricultural products and products of light industry such as processed food, textiles, metal products, and machinery for export (Liu 1969).

Death rates fell in Taiwan after World War II from eighteen per thousand in 1947 to eight in 1956, mostly because of the import of Western technology, particularly antibiotics. Birth rates began to decline in the late 1950s and then dropped precipitously. In 1964 the TFR was 5.10, and by 1985, it was at a below replacement level of 1.89 (Chang 2003). Urban women were the first to limit fertility, but rural areas lagged behind cities by only 7–9 years. Most of the decline was due to a decline in marital fertility, followed by a rising age at first marriage. As in Japan, there was an increase in the number

Status and fertility in East Asia 59

of people unmarried. In 1960 only 1% of Taiwanese women aged 45–54 were unmarried, and by the year 2000 this had reached 4.2% (Jones 2005). The trend has been less pronounced for Taiwanese men. Of Taiwanese men aged 45–54, in 1960 5.6% of men were unmarried, and by 2000 this was 5.9%. More recently, continued fertility decline has been due to increasing age at marriage and nonmarriage (Chang 2003, p. 614) as well as increasing childlessness (Sobotka 2021).

As in Japan, in all regions, highly educated women were the first to limit their fertility. So in 1966 a woman with a college degree was likely to have 2.5 children, a woman with a primary school education was likely to have 4.60 children. By 1983 there was less of a discrepancy – a woman with a college degree was likely to have 1.64 children, on average, while a woman with a primary school education was likely to have 2.83 children. Also as in Japan, education reduces female fertility more than male fertility. This is because the least-educated men are less likely to marry and therefore remain childless. For those born in 1966–1970, more highly educated men were more likely to be married than less educated men (Chen & Chen 2014). The trend is opposite for women – more highly educated women are more likely to remain single. For example, in 2012 only 16.3% of Taiwanese men with a college degree were single, while 26% of women with a college degree were single.

Korea

In South Korea a similar process occurred. There was rapid industrialization in the period after the Korean War, aided by a flood of international aid. South Korea was transformed from a primarily rural and agricultural nation where most people lived in the country to a mostly urban and industrial one where most people lived in the city. As in Taiwan, the introduction of Western medical technology greatly reduced mortality especially among children and infants. Mortality declined steeply. The government began family planning programs in 1962, but by this time fertility change had already begun. TFR fell from over 6 in 1960 to below replacement in 1985, about the same time as in Taiwan (Lim 2021).

After the Korean War there was government-led expansion of access to education. Compulsory primary education was introduced in 1954. Particularly after the 1960s, women's access to education increased dramatically. Of women born in 1960, few women graduated from high school, but by the 1970 birth cohort more than 95% had graduated from high school. More women who graduated also went on to attend college. In 1980 only 22.2% of all female high school graduates went to college, but by the late 2000s, 80% of female high school graduates did.

As in other East Asian countries, it is the more highly educated women who led the way in Korea's fertility decline. Yoo (2014) found that for women born earlier in the 20th century, the college educated had the lowest fertility,

60   *Status and fertility in East Asia*

while in more recent birth cohorts with below replacement fertility, the difference in fertility has all but disappeared.

For men, the college educated also had low fertility earlier in the transition, but more recently this seems to be changing. For example, Kim (2008) finds in a study of married women's fertility using the Korean National Fertility Survey that women who married more highly educated men before the 1997 Asian economic crisis had lower fertility, while women who married more highly educated men after the 1997 economic crisis had higher fertility. The pattern is similar for occupational status: before the crisis the wives of men in higher-status, white-collar occupations had fewer children than the wives of manual workers, while after the crisis the wives of men in the more prestigious occupations have tended to have higher fertility than the wives of agricultural workers and laborers.

As in much of the rest of East Asia, there has been a retreat from marriage in Korea and an increase in childlessness. Jones (2005) finds that from 1960 to 2000 the proportion of women unmarried by age 45–49 rose from 0.1% to 1.7%; for men, the increase was from 0.2% to 2.4%. As in Japan, unmarried men are disproportionately poorer and less educated, as home ownership and employment security are particularly important for male marriage. Data also show that higher socioeconomic status including income, education, and security of employment status are now positively associated with fertility for Korean men (Raymo et al. 2015; Lim 2021).

China

Mortality rates began to fall in China in some regions as early as the 17th century, about the same time as in Europe, although as is typical in the demographic transition, at first fertility rates stayed high. As a result, the population grew rapidly over the centuries and China became the most populous country in the world. After the 20th century upheavals of World War II and the Communist Revolution, the Communist government of Mao Tse Tung set about industrializing the country, which it achieved to some extent, although development in China was far slower than in neighboring Korea, Japan, and Taiwan. As China industrialized, per capita incomes rose and with it, life expectancy increased and infant mortality declined. As death rates fell, life expectancy at birth rose from an estimated 24 years of age in 1929 to about 40 years in 1953 (Banister 1984). The Great Leap Forward of 1958–1962 and the forced collectivization of agriculture led to a shrinking of the economy and reduced some of these gains. There was widespread famine, death rates spiked upward, and there were between 20 and 30 million excess deaths. By the mid-1960s economic growth had resumed again and mortality rates regained their downward trajectory. By 1970 life expectancy at birth had risen to about 61 years of age, and was 65 years of age in 1980.

The economic growth of China accelerated in the late 1970s. The 1978 economic reforms under the new leader Deng Xiaoping first led to a doubling of the production of grain, while real incomes more than doubled in the villages and increased by about 65% in the cities in the 1980s (Walder 1989). There was a further development of industry, much of it catering to the export market. Between 1992 and 2012 the gross domestic product of China increased at an average pace of 9% per year (Xu et al. 2014).

After a brief increase in fertility after the Great Leap Forward, the transition to low fertility in China began in the mid-1960s. Fertility fell rapidly in the 1970s and 1980s, and reached below replacement level by 1990. The "one child policy" family planning program was introduced by the government in 1979 and helped speed the pace of change. The government also expanded access to education for both men and women. In 1986 China implemented the 9-year compulsory education law, although the law took effect in different provinces at different times. This made 6 years of primary school and 3 years of junior high school both compulsory and free for all school-age children in China (Chen & Guo 2022). As a result the junior high enrolment rate in China rose from 68.3% in 1981 to 99.2% in 2005. The result was a huge rise in literacy in China. Using data from the first and second waves of the Chinese Family Panel Studies (CFPS) in 2010 and 2012, Xu et al. (2014) find that among marriages formed before 1970, 47% of husbands and 76% of wives were illiterate. For marriages between 2000 and 2012, only 7.5% of husbands and 9.9% of wives were illiterate.

As in Japan, Korea, and Taiwan, more educated men and women led the way in fertility decline (Freedman et al. 1988). Freedman et al. (1988) studied two provinces, Sichuan and Liaoning, using data from the One-per-Thousand Survey of 1982, which collected information on individual reproductive histories and educational attainment for women aged 15–49 in the period 1967–1970 (before the economic reforms) and 1979–1981 (after the economic reforms). These provinces were very different. In 1982 Liaoning was among the most economically developed provinces in China and was 42% urban; Sichuan was one of the least economically developed provinces and was only 14% urban. Liaoning was also considerably richer than Sichuan. Rural incomes per capita in Liaoning in 1982 exceeded those of Sichuan by 60%. People in Liaoning were more educated than people in Sichuan: in 1982 only 27% of adult females were illiterate in rural Liaoning compared to 47% in Sichuan.

In the richer Liaoning province, before the economic reforms from 1967 to 1970, more highly educated women had fewer children. For the province as a whole TFRs were 5.7 for illiterate women, 4.5 for women with a primary school education, and 3.3 for women with a junior high school education or higher. This negative relationship between education and fertility was particularly true in rural areas. In urban areas fertility rates were much lower (an average TFR across all groups of about 3.0) and there was no negative relationship between education and fertility. From 1979 to 1982, after the economic reforms, fertility rates had declined but the negative relationship between fertility and education persisted. For the entire

62 *Status and fertility in East Asia*

province TFRs were now 2.9 for illiterate women, 2.3 for women with a primary school education, and 1.7 for women with a junior high school education or higher. By now in urban areas, however, women with higher education had a higher TFR than women with lower education. Most of the decline in fertility in Liaoning was due to declines of fertility within marriage, rather than a change in proportions married or rising educational levels.

More educated women also had lower fertility in the poorer and less economically developed Sichuan province. In 1967 to 1970, before the economic reforms, the average TFRs for the entire province were 6.9 for illiterate women, 5.8 for women with a primary school education, and 3.9 for women with a junior high school education or higher. Fertility rates were lower in urban areas, but the same negative correlation between education and fertility was evident. From 1979 to 1982, after the economic reforms, TFRs were much lower although there was still a negative relationship between education and fertility. For the entire province TFRs were 2.6 for illiterate women, 2.1 for women with a primary school education, and 1.7 for women with a junior high school education or higher. While there was still a negative correlation between education and fertility for women in rural areas, now in urban areas the negative correlation between education and fertility had reversed and become a positive correlation. As in Liaoning, most of the decline in fertility in Sichuan between the two periods was due to a decline of fertility within marriage, and a much smaller part was due to the decline in marriage rates (Freedman et al. 1988).

In both these provinces in the late 1960s and early 1980s, more educated women were most likely to delay marriage, but the negative association between education and marriage was slight since marriage was nearly universal, as was true in most of China. In recent years the negative association between education and chance of marriage for women has increased. A study of urban Chinese born since 1974 shows that it is the most highly educated women who are least likely to marry (Yu & Xie 2015; You et al. 2021). Yu and Xie (2021) estimate that for urban women born in the 1970s, about 10% of women with a graduate education remain single. Since few women have children outside of marriage, this means that it is the most highly educated women who are most likely to remain childless. Chen and Guo (2022) used data from a random sample of the 2010 Chinese Census and found that more education significantly increased the probability of a woman remaining childless. Their study also was able to exploit the regional and time variations in the enforcement of compulsory schooling (which made 9 years of schooling compulsory) to show that the increased education of women permanently reduced fertility, but mostly by reducing the number of children born per woman rather than increasing the incidence of childlessness. They found that women who were exposed to the compulsory education law of 1986 had fewer children, such that an additional year of female education reduced the number of children by 0.24. The negative effect of increased women's education was larger among women living in rural areas than among urban women.

Once again the negative relationship between education and fertility is less for men than for women, as it is the least-educated men who are most likely to never marry (Yu & Xie 2021). This has become particularly true since the economic reforms of the 1970s. Before the reforms the return to education was low in Chinese society, and people and their families were more likely to choose marriage partners based on their family origin, party membership, work unit, or urban status rather than their education. After the reforms, the economic returns to education increased and education became a primary consideration when choosing a marriage partner (Xu et al. 2014). Higher education has particularly improved men's marriage prospects. There is an increasing trend toward women marrying men with a similar or higher level of education to themselves (Xu et al. 2014). Ownership of housing has also become an important prerequisite for marriage for men. These trends mean that poorly educated, low-income men are least likely to marry. The marriage squeeze for the least-educated men has been exacerbated by artificially high sex ratios due to son preference and disproportionate abortion of female fetuses in China in conjunction with the one child policy. Data from a study of Chinese mini census and survey data from 2003 and 2008 show the prevalence of nonmarriage became as high as one-quarter for urban men born since 1974 with very low levels of education (Yu & Xie 2015), and these unmarried men are very unlikely to have children, as there is a virtual absence of nonmarital childbearing in China (Yu & Xie 2021).

Zhang and Santtila (2022), on the basis of the General Social Survey of China conducted between 2010 and 2017 (n = 55,875 men and 28,931 women), found that higher standardized income and education level (standardized according to respondent's region, sex, and year of the survey) were associated with more children only for men, mainly because better educated, high-income men have a lower risk of remaining childless and are more frequently in more stable relationships. For women, on the contrary, as is found in other parts of the world, higher social status (in terms of income and education) lowers the likelihood to find a mate and thus lowers reproductive success. Further, the relative status between spouses also affected the couple's reproduction as couples had on average more children if the husband had a higher status than the wife (Zhang & Santtila 2022).

In sum, in the societies of East Asia that have completed their demographic transitions and are now low mortality, low fertility societies, there was a well- documented negative relationship between status (particularly as measured by education and occupational status) and fertility, just as there was in Europe and America. In all these countries transitioning from high fertility rates to low fertility rates, it was the more educated individuals in white-collar jobs in the new industrial economies who led the way in fertility decline. Evidence on male fertility is much less abundant than evidence on female fertility. This evidence suggests from East Asia that the negative

64 *Status and fertility in East Asia*

relationship between education and fertility has been smaller for men than for women, primarily because education is positively associated with income and occupational status, and income and occupational status have remained important for marriage for men in all countries.

Yet, more recently, differences in fertility by level of education and occupational status have shrunk in East Asia for both men and women. Given a retreat from marriage and very low levels of fertility in East Asia, there is in fact evidence of an emerging positive relationship between education, occupational status, income, and fertility, mostly for men. As we will see in Chapter 8, this is also the trend in much of Europe and America.

References

Atoh, M. (2008). Japan's population growth during the last 100 years. In F. Coulmas, H. Conrad, A. Schad-Seifert, & G. Vogt (Eds), *The demographic challenge: A handbook about Japan* (p. 5). Leiden: Brill.

Atoh, M., Kandiah, V., & Ivanov, S. (2004). The second demographic transition in Asia? Comparative analysis of the low fertility situation in East and South-East Asian countries. *Japanese Journal of Population*, 2(1), 42–75.

Banister, J. (1984). An analysis of recent data on the population of China. *Population and Development Review*, 241–271.

Bronfenbrenner, M. (1961). Some lessons of Japan's economic development, 1853–1938. *Pacific Affairs*, 34(1), 7–27.

Chang, M. C. (2003). Demographic transition in Taiwan. *Journal of Population and Social Security*, 1, 611–628.

Chen, J., & Guo, J. (2022). The effect of female education on fertility: Evidence from China's compulsory schooling reform. *Economics of Education Review*, 88, 102257.

Chen, Y. H., & Chen, H. (2014). Continuity and changes in the timing and formation of first marriage among postwar birth cohorts in Taiwan. *Journal of Family Issues*, 35(12), 1584–1604.

Freedman, R., Zhenyu, X., Bohua, L., & Lavely, W. (1988). Education and fertility in two Chinese provinces: 1967–1970 to 1979–1982. *Asia-Pacific Population Journal*, 3(1), 3–30.

Ghaznavi, C., Sakamoto, H., Yamasaki, L., Nomura, S., Yoneoka, D., Shibuya, K., & Ueda, P. (2022). Salaries, degrees, and babies: Trends in fertility by income and education among Japanese men and women born 1943–1975 – analysis of national surveys. *PLoS One*, 17(4), e0266835.

Jones, G. W. (2005). The "flight from marriage" in South-East and East Asia. *Journal of Comparative Family Studies*, 36(1), 93–119.

Kim, D. S. (2008). The 1997 Asian economic crisis and changes in the pattern of socioeconomic differentials in Korean fertility. In G. Jones, P. T. Straughan, & A. Chan (Eds), *Ultra-Low Fertility in Pacific Asia* (pp. 128–149). London: Routledge.

Lim, Sojung. (2021). Socioeconomic differentials in fertility in South Korea. *Demographic Research*, 44(39), 941–978.

Liu, T. C. (1969). The process of industrialization in Taiwan. *Developing Economies*, 7(1), 63–80.

O'Bryan, S. (2009). *The growth idea: Purpose and prosperity in postwar Japan.* Honolulu: University of Hawaii Press.

Ogawa, N., Retherford, R. D., & Matsukura, R. (2009). Japan's declining fertility and policy responses. In G. Jones, P. T. Straughan, & A. Chan (Eds), *Ultra-low fertility in Pacific Asia* (pp. 58–90). London: Routledge..

Piotrowski, M., Kalleberg, A., & Rindfuss, R. R. (2015). Contingent work rising: Implications for the timing of marriage in Japan. *Journal of Marriage and Family*, 77(5), 1039–1056.

Raymo, J. M., Park, H., Xie, Y., & Yeung, W. J. J. (2015). Marriage and family in East Asia: Continuity and change. *Annual Review of Sociology*, 41, 471–492.

Roser M. (2014). Fertility Rate. Our world in Data. https://ourworldindata.org/fertility-rate First published in 2014; substantive revision published on December 2, 2017. Last Time Accessed 19. Nov. 2023.

Shirahase, S. (2000). Women's increased higher education and the declining fertility rate in Japan. *Review of Population and Social Policy*, 9(2000), 47–63.

Skirbekk, V. (2022). *Decline and prosper!: Changing global birth rates and the advantages of fewer children.* Cham: Springer Nature.

Sobotka, T. (2021). World's highest childlessness levels in East Asia. *Population Societies*, 595(11), 1–4.

Tsuya, N. O. (2023). Educational attainment, first employment, and first marriage in Japan. *Journal of Family Issues*, 0(0), 1–24. https://doi.org/10.1177/0192513X231155594

Walder, A. G. (1989). Social change in post-revolution China. *Annual Review of Sociology*, 15(1), 405–424.

Xu, Q., Li, J., & Yu, X. (2014). Continuity and change in Chinese marriage and the family: Evidence from the CFPS. *Chinese Sociological Review*, 47(1), 30–56.

Yoo, Sam Hyun. (2014). Educational differentials in cohort fertility during the fertility transition in South Korea. *Demographic Research*, 30(Jan–June), 1463–1494.

Yu, J., & Xie, Y. (2015). Changes in the determinants of marriage entry in post-reform urban China. *Demography*, 52(6), 1869–92.

Yu, J., & Xie, Y. (2021). Recent trends in the Chinese family. *Demographic Research*, 44, 595–608.

You, J., Yi, X., & Chen, M. (2021). Love, life, and "leftover ladies" in urban China: Staying modernly single in patriarchal traditions. *China Economic Review*, 68, 101626.

Zhang, Y., & Santtila, P. (2022). Social status predicts different mating and reproductive success for men and women in China: evidence from the 2010–2017 CGSS data. *Behavioral Ecology and Sociobiology*, 76(7), 101.

7 Status and fertility in contemporary transitioning societies

As has been described in Chapter 5, the demographic transition in a country or region usually consists of four stages: (1) high mortality and high fertility together, (2) a period of mortality decline, (3) a period of fertility decline, and (4) low mortality and low fertility in a new equilibrium (Skirbekk 2022). As we saw in Chapters 5 and 6, this transition was more or less complete by the end of the 20th century in Europe, the former European settler colonies including America, and much of East Asia, including China. The transition has now either occurred or at least begun all over the world (Dyson & Murphy 1985; Bongaarts & Hodgson 2022).

While individual countries have followed very different historical trajectories in this process and each has had a different speed and timing of fertility decline, just as in Europe and East Asia, in currently transitioning countries fertility decline has generally accompanied increasing industrialization, urbanization, gross domestic product, education of the population, and decreases in the child mortality rate (see Figure 7.1).

In all countries and in all regions, including Africa, the two most important factors in fertility decline are an increasing level of education of the population and a decreasing child mortality rate (Bongaarts & Hodgson 2022, p. 53). As a result of fertility declines, in most countries the process of rapid population growth characteristic of stage two of the demographic transition has come to an end and has already begun to reverse as fertility rates have fallen and countries have entered stage four of the transition. Today global fertility has declined to below three births per woman (Bongaarts & Hodgson 2022).

Yet there are still many countries in the world today that have not fully completed their demographic transitions. These countries include countries in Africa, the Middle East, Southeast Asia, and South America (see the list in Table 7.1). The differences in total fertility rates (TFRs; or the number of children born to the average woman) between these countries is large. Yet, despite this, nearly all the countries in the list did experience a significant drop in fertility during the last few decades. The most prominent exception is Africa south of the Sahara, although even here birth rates did decrease to some extent (see Figure 7.2). In some sub-Saharan African countries, a

DOI: 10.4324/9781003463320-7

Status and fertility in contemporary transitioning societies 67

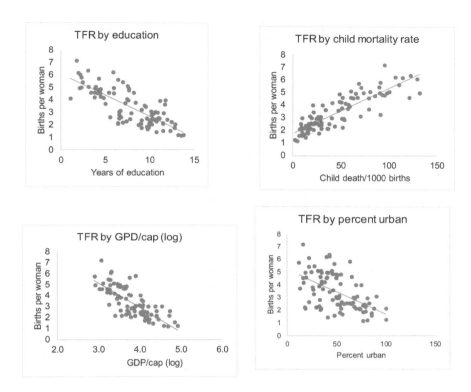

Figure 7.1 Total fertility rate by socioeconomic indicators for 97 developing countries in 2015.

Source: From Bongaarts and Hodgson (2022, p. 53) and licensed under the terms of the Creative Commons Attribution 4.0 International License (http://creativecommons.org/licenses/by/4.0/).

stalled demographic transition (lower mortality, but continued high fertility) has led to a substantial increase in the population (Bongaarts & Hodgson 2022; Skirbekk 2022). As a result, the U.N. predicts that Africa will contain 40% of the world's population by the end of the century (Bongaarts & Hodgson 2022).

Status and fertility in contemporary developing countries

What do we know of the relationship between individual status and fertility in countries that are still in the process of demographic transition? Although we often know more about fertility in contemporary transitioning societies than in historical societies, we continue to know very little about sex differences in the effects of status on fertility. Most studies of fertility continue to examine the fertility of women only, often at the aggregate level. In

68 *Status and fertility in contemporary transitioning societies*

Table 7.1 Total fertility rate per women (selected countries): time series from 1960 until 2020 for some selected developing countries

Country Name	1960	1970	1980	1990	2000	2010	2020
Afghanistan	7.45	7.45	7.45	7.47	7.49	5.98	4.18
Angola	6.71	7.43	7.46	7.27	6.64	6.19	5.37
Arab World	6.98	6.92	6.34	5.19	3.85	3.47	3.15
Burundi	6.94	7.25	7.40	7.41	6.92	6.18	5.24
Benin	6.28	6.75	7.03	6.74	5.96	5.36	4.70
Bangladesh	6.73	6.95	6.36	4.50	3.17	2.32	1.99
Belize	6.50	6.30	5.85	4.51	3.60	2.69	2.25
Bolivia	6.36	6.00	5.47	4.89	4.05	3.21	2.65
Côte d'Ivoire	7.69	7.94	7.59	6.62	5.87	5.09	4.54
Cameroon	5.65	6.20	6.63	6.44	5.58	5.11	4.44
Congo, Dem. Rep.	6.00	6.22	6.54	6.75	6.75	6.54	5.72
Colombia	6.74	5.28	3.86	3.08	2.57	1.99	1.77
Djibouti	6.46	6.80	6.55	6.07	4.48	3.30	2.63
Algeria	7.52	7.64	6.79	4.73	2.51	2.86	2.94
Ecuador	6.72	6.14	4.73	3.74	3.10	2.62	2.38
Egypt, Arab Rep.	6.72	6.23	5.61	4.58	3.34	3.23	3.24
Eritrea	6.90	6.65	6.67	6.50	5.32	4.57	3.93
Ethiopia	6.88	6.98	7.32	7.25	6.54	5.14	4.05
Gabon	4.38	5.08	5.68	5.44	4.53	4.15	3.87
Ghana	6.75	6.95	6.54	5.60	4.83	4.27	3.77
Guinea	6.11	6.24	6.53	6.60	6.08	5.34	4.55
Gambia, The	6.25	6.19	6.38	6.10	5.88	5.58	5.09
Indonesia	5.67	5.47	4.43	3.12	2.51	2.48	2.27
India	5.91	5.59	4.83	4.05	3.31	2.58	2.18
Iran, Islamic Rep.	6.93	6.44	6.48	4.69	2.07	1.84	2.14
Iraq	6.25	7.36	6.57	5.88	4.94	4.34	3.54
Liberia	6.41	6.70	6.97	6.50	5.87	4.97	4.18
Libya	7.20	8.13	7.22	4.97	2.85	2.48	2.18
Morocco	7.04	6.65	5.69	4.05	2.77	2.57	2.35

Status and fertility in contemporary transitioning societies   69

Madagascar	7.30	7.27	6.73	6.18	5.55	4.60	3.98
Mali	6.97	7.13	7.15	7.17	6.90	6.55	5.69
Mongolia	6.95	7.57	6.21	4.05	2.14	2.64	2.83
Niger	7.45	7.57	7.84	7.77	7.68	7.47	6.74
Nigeria	6.35	6.47	6.78	6.49	6.11	5.84	5.25
Nicaragua	7.37	6.86	6.14	4.60	3.11	2.60	2.35
Oman	7.25	7.31	8.30	7.17	3.72	2.87	2.78
Pakistan	6.60	6.60	6.53	6.16	5.04	3.95	3.39
Peru	6.94	6.32	5.04	3.91	2.85	2.55	2.21
Philippines	7.15	6.26	5.18	4.32	3.81	3.18	2.49
Papua New Guinea	6.28	6.16	5.69	4.80	4.53	3.99	3.48
Paraguay	6.50	5.74	5.17	4.55	3.55	2.73	2.38
Rwanda	8.19	8.23	8.46	7.18	5.64	4.52	3.93
Sudan	6.69	6.89	6.80	6.15	5.47	4.88	4.29
Senegal	7.00	7.26	7.29	6.45	5.45	5.06	4.49
Sierra Leone	6.13	6.50	6.69	6.72	6.32	5.20	4.08
Somalia	7.25	7.18	7.01	7.40	7.63	6.87	5.89
Tanzania	6.81	6.77	6.65	6.21	5.69	5.43	4.77
Uganda	7.00	7.12	7.10	7.09	6.87	6.11	4.70
South Africa	6.04	5.67	4.98	3.96	2.69	2.60	2.36
Yemen, Rep.	7.94	8.39	8.71	8.61	6.31	4.67	3.61
Zimbabwe	7.16	7.42	6.87	4.86	3.75	4.03	3.46

Source: World Bank data, https://data.worldbank.org/indicator/SP.DYN.TFRT.IN.

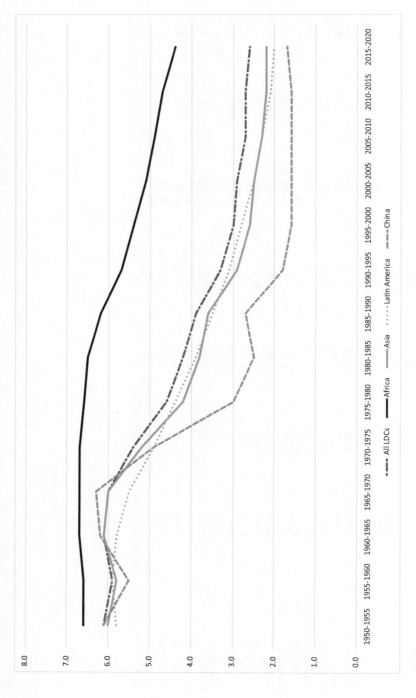

Figure 7.2 Total fertility rate of the developing world, by region 1950–2020.

Source: (UN Population Division 2019); from Bongaarts and Hodgson (2022, p. 5) and licensed under the terms of the Creative Commons Attribution 4.0 International License (http://creativecommons.org/licenses/by/4.0/).

Status and fertility in contemporary transitioning societies 71

those studies that do examine the relationship between status and fertility at the individual level, in transitioning societies, education, income, and occupational status are widely used as measures of individual status just as they are in societies that have completed their demographic transition (Skirbekk 2008). Of these, the relationship between education (particularly of women) and fertility is best documented.

Education and fertility

Education has been recognized by most demographers as one of the most important, if not the most important, predictors of the worldwide decrease in fertility (Skirbekk 2022). In all countries, more highly educated women have led the way in fertility decline as they have in all the societies with completed transitions examined in Chapter 6 (Ashurst et al. 1984; Martin 1995). For example, in Bangladesh, data from 1945 to 1965 show the lowest fertility for women in the highest educational group, and this negative relationship persists into the contemporary period (Bora et al. 2022; Haq et al. 2023). In India, the second most populous society in the world, there has recently been a drop in overall fertility to below replacement levels. Yet this low overall fertility rate masks much variation among socioeconomic groups, with highly educated women having the lowest fertility. According to the Indian National Family Health Survey, in 2022 women with no education in India had a TFR of 2.8, and women with 12 or more years of schooling had a TFR of 1.8. (In Seven, 2022).

In the Middle East and Turkey, it is the educated and urban elite as well as certain religious groups that have spearheaded fertility decline (Drioui et al. 2022). For example, data from the World Fertility Survey show that in Jordan, Syria, Yemen, and Turkey in the 1980s, women with over 7 years of schooling had lower total fertility than their peers with no education (TFRs of 4.9 vs 9.3 in Jordan, 4.1 vs 8.8 in Syria, 5.4 vs 8.6 in Yemen, and 2.07 vs 5.91 in Turkey).

In Latin America, overall fertility has fallen from a pre-transition average of 6.7 in the late 1960s and 1970s to 2.2 in 2020 (Bongaarts & Hodgson 2022). Better off and more educated women have been the first to limit fertility in Latin America. For example, in the 1980s the highest educated women in Columbia, Ecuador, Paraguay, Peru, and Venezuela always had lower fertility than the least-educated women, with TFRs around 3 for the highest educated and 7 or 8 for the least educated (Ashurst et al. 1984). This trend continues to the present day. For example, in Chile, Enríquez et al. (2022) use data from a cohort of 6,802 Chilean women born between 1961 and 1970 and finds that Chilean women of high socioeconomic status (a measure that includes education) have later ages at first birth, earlier ages at last birth, and fewer children than women of lower socioeconomic status.

Countries in Southeast Asia include Indonesia, Brunei, Malaysia, Philippines, Thailand, Cambodia, Laos, Myanmar, Singapore, and

72 Status and fertility in contemporary transitioning societies

Timor-Leste. In 1960, most countries in Southeast Asia had TFRs around 5 to 7, but they had all dropped to below 3 by 2014, with the exception of Timor-Leste. Singapore largely followed the East Asian pattern, with the TFR falling to below replacement by 1975 (Yeung 2022). The same pattern of better-educated women being the first to limit their fertility is seen in Southeast Asia as in other parts of the world (Ashurst et al. 1984). Better-educated women in these countries continue to have lower fertility than other women, in part because they are less likely to ever marry and have children (Jones 2009, p. 25).

In Sub-Saharan Africa, TFRs have fallen from highs of 7.1 pre-transition to 4.4 in 2020 (Bongaarts & Hodgson 2022). Once again, educated women were the first to limit their fertility, beginning in the 1970s. Unlike other countries, however, fertility differences between the better educated and least educated have not converged in many Sub-Saharan countries and in fact have substantially widened from the 1990s to about 2010, as fertility rates continued to decline among better educated women while they stopped declining among other groups (Corker et al. 2022). There are exceptions to this pattern. In Ghana, for example, from 1993 to 2014, the TFR in Ghana decreased from 5.50 to 4.15, but while fertility rates fell for most women during these years, the TFR for the most-educated group has actually increased (Agbaglo et al. 2022).

A primary reason why higher education is associated with lower fertility particularly among women (Mills et al. 2011) is that it is associated with a later onset of reproduction and a higher age at first birth, as noted in Chapter 5. A more indirect effect that may be particularly relevant in contemporary developing countries could be that education may modify an individual's prospect of life, changing values, and, importantly, providing women with more opportunities for autonomous decisions on fertility. Impressive data on differences in fertility between educated and noneducated women from Ethiopia, for instance, emphasize the importance of the latter for women in the developing world (Hailemariam 2017). Additionally, women with higher levels of education may also be more likely to invest in their own children's education, increasing the period of time in which the children are dependent on their parents (Angrist et al. 2005) and making the upbringing of each child more expensive (Becker 2009). Thus, more highly educated women may be more likely to think they cannot afford to have too many children.

Income, wealth, and fertility

Income data from transitioning societies are mostly collected for households, and as a result sex differences in the effects of personal income on fertility are often blurred (Fieder et al. 2011). If analyzed on the level of populations

Status and fertility in contemporary transitioning societies 73

and if data on the number of children are not separately available for men and for women but only data for women have been recorded, the association between household income and fertility is negative – the higher the wealth, the lower is the fertility (Skirbekk 2022).

In most countries where the demographic transition is still in progress, there is also a negative relationship between the occupational status of the husband and the wife's fertility, as was the case in transitioning Europe and Asia. For example, in the Middle East, in the 1980s the wives of educated white-collar and professional men had lower fertility than the wives of farmers (the TFRs were 6.9 vs 9.2 in Jordan, 7.9 vs 9.4 in Syria, 7.3 vs 7.9 in Yemen, and 3.7 vs 5.4 in Turkey). This was also true in many South American countries (Ashurst et al. 1984). In Uruguay, the TFR fell from 2.5 to 1.9 children between 1996 and 2011 (Nathan et al. 2016), with women of middle to high socioeconomic status postponing births and having fewer births than women in lower social strata. Similarly in Chile, in 2013, women of higher socioeconomic status had later ages of first birth and fewer children than women of lower socioeconomic status (as measured by household income, education, and health variables – see Enriquez et al. 2022).

While socioeconomic factors also tend to be negatively associated with fertility for men in currently transitioning countries, the association is usually less for men. For example, to examine the relationship between income and fertility for men, Fieder et al. (2011) analyzed census data from Brazil, Mexico, Panama, South Africa, and Venezuela (totaling ~9 million cases for years since 2000) provided by IPUMS international, and used the absence of children in the household as a proxy for childlessness (as no data on actual number of children for men are provided by those census data). Income was measured as personal income from all sources. They found that the highest income males were most likely to be married and the least likely to be childless. They also found that the highest income females were least likely to be married and most likely to be childless. Thus, in these countries quite similar to developed countries, a higher proportion of low-income men than high-income men remain unmarried and childless (Fieder et al. 2011, Hopcroft 2021). As in many developed countries, a lower percentage of low-income men are selected into marriage in developing countries. This also suggests that personal income as a proxy for social status for men is universally valid and largely independent of the culture, and that, worldwide, men with low income are more likely to drop out of reproduction than other men.

Furthermore, using data from married couples from countries as diverse as Brazil, Colombia, Dominican Republic, Indonesia, Israel, Mexico, Panama, South Africa, and Venezuela (in total 791,966 couples), Fieder and Huber (2020) demonstrated that a wife's probability of remaining childless decreased with the increasing income of her husband but increased with her own increasing income. Overall, they found that both wife's and husband's

74 *Status and fertility in contemporary transitioning societies*

income were significantly negatively associated with wife's number of children. Only in Israel was there a positive association between husband's income and wife's number of children. Yet in contrast to the other analyzed countries, Israel is a post-demographic transition society, and there is evidence that in post-demographic transitions there is a positive association between husband's income and wife's number of children (Hopcroft 2022). As we note in Chapter 8, it is likely that the positive effect of male (and also female) status on the number of children emerges after a completed demographic transition.

To conclude, while the demographic transition or the transition from high fertility to low fertility has now taken place to some extent in all countries of the world, the timing and extent of the fall in fertility differs from country to country. However, in all countries it is highly educated women who have been the first to limit their fertility. In most societies in mid-transition, there is a negative relationship between various measures of status, including education and income, and fertility. Yet despite this, social status for men remains important for being selected into marriage and having any children at all. Thus available data from developing countries indicate that mate selection criteria and thus their influence on reproduction appear to be to some degree similar all over the world (Buss 1989; Shackelford et al. 2005). Furthermore, women with a higher-income spouse are least likely to be childless. Yet the societies examined in this chapter have not finished their demographic transitions. In these societies income in particular may only recently be a major source of status and other factors such as land ownership may play a more important role in marriage and family formation, yet land ownership is not a factor included in most of the available surveys. More reliable data on individual and culturally appropriate data on social status as well as offspring count separately for men and women are urgently needed.

References

Agbaglo, E., Agbadi, P., Tetteh, J. K., Ameyaw, E. K., Adu, C., & Nutor, J. J. (2022). Trends in total fertility rate in Ghana by different inequality dimensions from 1993 to 2014. *BMC Women's Health*, 22(1), 1–8.

Angrist, J., Lavy, V., & Schlosser, A. (2005). New evidence on the causal link between the quantity and quality of children. NBER Working Paper Series. Working Paper 11835, from www.nber.org/papers/w11835. Last accessed November 20th, 2023.

Ashurst, H., Balkaran, S., & Casterline, J. B. (1984). Socio-economic differentials in recent fertility. Voorburg, Netherlands: International Statistical Institute.

Becker, G. S. (2009). *Human capital: A theoretical and empirical analysis, with special reference to education*. Chicago: University of Chicago Press.

Bongaarts, J., & Hodgson, D. (2022). *Fertility transition in the developing world*. Springer Nature. ISBN: 978-3-031-11839-5.

Status and fertility in contemporary transitioning societies   75

Bora, J. K., Saikia, N., Kebede, E. B., & Lutz, W. (2022). Revisiting the causes of fertility decline in Bangladesh: The relative importance of female education and family planning programs. *Asian Population Studies*, 1–24.

Buss, D. M. (1989). Sex differences in human mate preferences: Evolutionary hypotheses tested in 37 cultures. *Behavioral and Brain Sciences*, 12(1), 1–14.

Corker, J., Rossier, C., & Zan, M. L. (2022). Fertility among better-off women in sub-Saharan Africa. *Demographic Research*, 46, 849–864.

Drioui, C., El Bidaoui, B., & Bakass, F. (2022). Diffusion test of fertility decline in Arab countries of the Middle East and North Africa (MENA) region. *Journal of Population and Social Studies*, 30, 562–590.

Dyson, T., & Murphy, M. (1985). The onset of fertility transition. *Population and Development Review*, 399–440.

Enríquez, Varas, P. J., McKerracher, L., & Montalva Rivera, N. (2022). Fertility dynamics and life history tactics vary by socioeconomic position in a transitioning cohort of postreproductive Chilean women. *Human Nature*, 33, 1–32.

Fieder, M., & Huber, S. (2020). Effects of wife's and husband's income on wife's reproduction: An evolutionary perspective on human mating. *Biodemography and Social Biology*, 65(1), 31–40.

Fieder, M., Huber, S., & Bookstein, F. L. (2011). Socioeconomic status, marital status and childlessness in men and women: An analysis of census data from six countries. *Journal of Biosocial Science*, 43(5), 619–635.

Hailemariam, A. (2017). The second biggest African country undergoing rapid change: Ethiopia. In H. Groth & F. May (Eds), *Africa's population: In search of a demographic dividend* (pp. 53–69). Cham: Springer. ASIN: B0719QWBZ2.

Haq, I., Hossain, M. I., Saleheen, A. A. S., Nayan, M. I., Afrin, T., & Talukder, A. (2023). Factors associated with women fertility in Bangladesh: Application on count regression models. *Current Women's Health Reviews*, 19(2), 26–37.

Hopcroft, R. L. (2021). High income men have high value as long-term mates in the US: Personal income and the probability of marriage, divorce, and childbearing in the US. *Evolution and Human Behavior*, 42(5), 409–417.

Hopcroft, R. L. (2022). Husband's income, wife's income, and number of biological children in the US. *Biodemography and Social Biology*, 67(1), 71–83.

In Seven Charts: India's Fertility Rate Drops Below Replacement. (2022). *The Times of India*, Retrieved September 18, 2023, from https://timesofindia.indiatimes.com/india/in-7-charts-indias-fertility-rate-drops-to-2-0-according-to-latest-national-family-health-*survey/articleshow/91373789.cms*.

Jones, G. W. (2009). Women, marriage and family in Southeast Asia. *Gender Trends in Southeast Asia: Women Now, Women in the Future*, 12–30.

Martin, T. C. (1995). Women's education and fertility: Results from 26 demographic and health surveys. *Studies in Family Planning*, 187–202.

Mills, M., Rindfuss, R. R., McDonald, P., Te Velde, E., & ESHRE Reproduction and Society Task Force. (2011). Why do people postpone parenthood? Reasons and social policy incentives. *Human Reproduction Update*, 17(6), 848–860.

Nathan, M., Pardo, I., & Cabella, W. (2016). Diverging patterns of fertility decline in Uruguay. *Demographic Research*, 34, 563–586.

Shackelford, T. K., Schmitt, D. P., & Buss, D. M. (2005). Universal dimensions of human mate preferences. *Personality and Individual Differences*, 39(2), 447–458.

76 *Status and fertility in contemporary transitioning societies*

Skirbekk, V. (2008). Fertility trends by social status. *Demographic Research*, 18, 145–180.

Skirbekk, V. (2022). *Decline and prosper!: Changing global birth rates and the advantages of fewer children.* Cham: Springer Nature.

United Nations. (2019). World population prospects 2019, Department of Economic and Social Affairs, Population Division, 141.

Yeung, W. J. J. (2022). *Demographic and family transition in Southeast Asia* (p. 112). Cham: Springer Nature.

8 The relationship between status and fertility in post-transition Europe and America

As a result of the demographic transition and continued falls in fertility rates, in many developed countries fertility rates are now below replacement level. For example, the current total fertility rate (a measure of how many children a woman is likely to have in her lifetime) in Germany (2020) is about one and a half children – much lower than the slightly over two children per woman that is considered a replacement level fertility rate. The same is true in Japan, Korea, Taiwan, and China. In such countries, the population is not replacing itself, and without in-migration to make up the difference, the population will shrink.

Many have argued that the lowest of the low fertility rates and below-replacement fertility contradict evolutionary theory. In societies with the falling fertility characteristic of the third stage of the demographic transition, as we have seen in Chapters 5–7, there is an inverse relationship between status and fertility, as elites lead the way in fertility change with lower fertility than nonelites. This is the opposite of the positive relationship between social status and fertility predicted by evolutionary theory. Yet all these societies undergoing the transition to low fertility are precisely that: societies in transition, with profound changes occurring in the nature of the way people earn their living, live their lives, and raise their families. As we noted in Chapter 2, evolutionary theory suggests that species-typical traits are much less likely to help individuals survive and reproduce in rapidly changing environments. Evolutionary theory is much more likely to apply to individuals in fairly stable environments. In this chapter, therefore, we look at the relationship between status and fertility in societies that are not rapidly changing and that have had relatively stable patterns of low fertility and low mortality for decades or more – in particular, the modern, developed societies of Europe and America.

As always, the measure of social status is specific to the society. We argue that status in modern societies for both men and women can usually be converted to money, which is transferable and convertible within a second almost anywhere in the world. Hence, personal income, assets, or wealth represent universal indicators of social status in modern market societies.

DOI: 10.4324/9781003463320-8

78 *Status and fertility in post-transition Europe and America*

Income and wealth are also direct measures of access to the material resources necessary for reproduction and childraising.

Yet income and wealth acquisition in modern societies typically require time-intensive investments in education and career. High-income jobs usually require high levels of education and/or long hours of work outside of the home, and both of these things can be difficult to combine with having many children. High levels of education usually mean postponement of family creation and thus a reduced time period available for childbearing, and long hours of intensive work can interfere with the everyday demands of childbearing and childraising. This is particularly the case for women, who have a shorter fertility window than do men and who usually face greater personal costs from childbearing and childraising than men do. Given this, and because evolutionary theory predicts that status will have a greater effect on male fertility than female fertility, in modern societies, personal income and wealth are likely to be direct predictors of fertility for men but are less likely to be so for women.

Previous studies of the relationship between status and fertility in contemporary societies often use education or occupational status as a measure of status. The trend toward using education as the measure of status has been particularly pronounced in recent years (Guzzo & Hayford 2020). As we saw in Chapters 5–7, use of education and occupational status as measures of status has also been the practice in studies of the relationship between status and fertility in transitioning societies. Yet, while education and occupational status are correlated with personal income and wealth, neither education nor occupational status alone guarantees a high level of personal income or wealth, and so in modern developed societies they are more of a prerequisite for income and wealth than anything else (Fieder & Huber 2022). Nevertheless, education and occupational status are clearly positively correlated with social status in modern societies. Given this and the nature of the available evidence, in this chapter we focus on two primary metrics of personal status – education and personal income. Because status is likely more important for men's fertility than women's fertility, and women typically face greater tradeoffs in income and wealth acquisition than do men, we examine the relationship between status and fertility for men and women separately. We also examine the effects of income and education for men and women within couples since childbearing and childraising typically takes place within the family.

Education and fertility

As we saw previously, the evidence from Europe, America, East Asia, and the rest of the world is that during the third stage of the demographic transition when fertility rates are falling in the country as a whole, the relationship between level of education and fertility for women is almost always negative, as the best educated women tend to have the fewest children. This negative

Status and fertility in post-transition Europe and America 79

relationship between education and fertility for women has persisted in all modern developed societies up to the present, although there is also some evidence that this is now changing, particularly in the richer regions of Europe, for the most recent cohorts of women.

For example, Nisén et al. (2021) find in a study of cohort fertility for women born in the late 1960s and early 1970s in 15 European countries (Austria, Belarus, Belgium, Finland, France, Germany, Greece, Hungary, Ireland, Lithuania, the Netherlands, Norway, Romania, Spain, and Sweden) that highly educated women in all countries have a lower average number of children than women with a low level of education, although the magnitude of the difference varies by country and ranges from negligible in Belgium (−0.01) to over one child difference in Romania (−1.01). They find that the more economically developed countries as measured by gross domestic product (e.g., Belgium, Norway) have smaller negative relationships between fertility and education for women than less economically developed countries (e.g., Romania, Hungary). They observe this trend across regions within countries as well as across countries.

In the most recent cohorts in Europe, there is in fact evidence that the negative relationship between education and fertility for women has actually become U-shaped or positive, particularly in the more economically developed regions of Western Europe (Kravdal & Rindfuss 2008; Jalovaara et al. 2019). A recent study of data for Belgium, Denmark, Finland, France, the Netherlands, Norway, and Sweden examined the probability of births by educational level for women aged 15–49, using data from 2001 to predict the chances of a birth in 2002–2005 (Wood et al. 2021). Women who were currently enrolled in education were excluded from the study. In all these societies, first births for women in higher educational categories were later than births for women in less educated categories. Yet there was a positive association between second births and education in most countries. In many Belgian, Danish, Dutch, and Norwegian regions, for third births there was a U-shaped pattern such that more highly educated women were more likely to have a third child than women with a medium level of education. Hudde and Engelhardt (2023) also found positive relationships between education and both marriage and children using census data for women in Germany between 1976 and 2019. This echoes the evidence of a change from a negative or flat relationship between education and fertility to a more positive relationship for women in recent years in East Asia, as noted in Chapter 6.

One of the reasons for the development of a positive relationship between education and fertility for women is rising childlessness among the low-educated (Brzozowska et al. 2022). The educational gradient in childlessness in Europe used to be strictly positive, such that more educated women were more likely to be childless (Beaujouan et al. 2016; van Bavel et al. 2018). However, in the 1950s birth cohorts it turned into a U-shaped one, with the lowest occurrence of childlessness among women with secondary education, in some of the Scandinavian countries (Andersson et al. 2009). More

80 *Status and fertility in post-transition Europe and America*

recently, childlessness rates among low-educated women have surpassed those among medium- and high-educated women in Denmark, Finland, Norway, and Sweden as well as many other low fertility countries (Jalovaara et al. 2019; Brzozowska et al. 2022). Brzozowska et al. (2022) found that among the 1960s birth cohorts, childlessness is highest among low-educated women in the Czech Republic, Russia, and Slovakia, and this pattern may be extended soon to Hungary, France, Italy, and Spain. In these countries the proportion of women without a secondary school education is very low and their employment prospects are poor. Further, they are often in tenuous relationships with men who have similar low levels of education and poor employment prospects. These factors tend to discourage fertility.

This emerging positive or U-shaped relationship between education and fertility for women in Europe does not seem to be replicated in the U.S. Studies by and large show a negative relationship between education and fertility for women in the U.S. (Hopcroft 2006, 2015; Guzzo & Hayford 2020), although the differences between women in completed fertility are small. In 2018, Census data on completed fertility show that women with less than a high school education had about 2.72 children, while women with a graduate or professional degree had about 1.82 children (U.S. Census Bureau 2018). This difference is not huge, but there is no indication of a positive relationship between status as measured by the highest degree received and fertility. Using U.S. data from the Wisconsin Longitudinal Study, Fieder and Huber (2022) find that a woman's education is significantly negatively associated with her number of children, with education explaining ~5% of the variance of the number of children. Similarly, using the 1979 National Longitudinal Survey of Youth (NLSY79) that followed youth who were in high school in 1979, Verweij et al. (2021) found that childlessness was more common among women who had higher levels of education. They found that about 9% of women who did not finish high school were childless, while about 29% of women with a postgraduate education were childless.

For men, as we also saw in previous chapters there is evidence that over the course of the demographic transition the relationship between education and fertility is also negative. This has changed in some countries in Europe. While in the U.S. and the U.K., education for men continues to be negatively associated with fertility (Hopcroft 2006, 2015; Nettle & Pollet 2008), education is now positively associated with fertility for men in northwestern Europe, in Finland (Nisén et al. 2013), Sweden (Fieder & Huber 2007), Germany (Hudde & Engelhardt 2023), and Norway (Lappegård & Rønsen 2013). Kaptijn et al. (2010) find evidence that occupational status, which is positively correlated with education level, is positively correlated with fertility as measured by the number of grandchildren for men in the Netherlands. As we saw in Chapter 6, there is also some evidence that the relationship between education and fertility for men in East Asia is also now positive.

Status and fertility in post-transition Europe and America   81

However, in all countries where a negative relationship between education and fertility exists, for men in statistical analyses the size of the relationship is generally smaller than it is for women (e.g., see Hopcroft 2015), in part because education is positively associated with personal income, and income tends to be positively associated with number of children for men, as we see below. Better educated men are also more likely to marry, which is an important precursor to childbearing, particularly in East Asia and to a lesser extent in Europe and America where there is more childbearing outside of marriage.

Personal income, wealth, and fertility

While education is a predictor of personal income, personal income and wealth are direct measures of the resources necessary for raising children in a modern society. Yet in both Europe and the U.S., the relationship between personal income and fertility for women is negative. This has been shown in the U.S. (Weeden et al. 2006; Hopcroft 2006, 2015, 2019; Stulp et al. 2016; Fieder & Huber 2021, 2022), the U.K. (Nettle & Pollet 2008), Norway (Lappegård & Rønsen 2013), Sweden (Fieder & Huber 2007; Goodman & Koupil 2010), and Finland (Nisén et al. 2018), although as with education the negative income fertility relationship for women is changing among recent cohorts in Scandinavia and becoming positive (e.g., Kravdal & Rindfuss 2008; Jalovaara et al. 2019; Kolk 2022).

In the U.S., where most (about 60%) of childbearing occurs within marriage, some of the negative relationship between personal income and fertility is because higher-income women are less likely to be married than other women. Fieder and Huber (2022) find, using a contemporary U.S. sample (Wisconsin Longitudinal Survey), that higher-income women have a slightly lower probability of ever being married. They find on the basis of U.S. census data that the negative association between personal income and ever married was higher in women aged 45–55 years in 1940 (income explaining 6% of the variance of ever married) than in 2019 (the variance explained is nearly zero; Fieder & Huber 2023). The declining relationship between personal income and marriage for women may be why Hopcroft (2021) using U.S. data from 2014 did not find that high-income women were less likely to ever marry than other women, although she found high-income women were less likely to remarry after divorce.

Yet likely most of the negative relationship between personal income and fertility for women in the U.S. represents tradeoffs women face between income earning and childbearing and raising. As a result, women with children are more likely to work part-time or not work at all than other women. For example, Verweij et al. (2021) find using longitudinal data from the 1979 National Longitudinal Survey of Youth (NLSY79) that women who did not work much in their lifetime were much less likely to be childless

82 *Status and fertility in post-transition Europe and America*

(about 7%) than women who worked outside of the home full-time all their lives (about 22%).

For men the relationship between personal income and fertility in all contemporary developed societies tends to be positive – higher-income men have more children on average than lower-income men. This positive relationship is found in the U.S. (Weeden et al. 2006; Hopcroft 2006, 2015, 2019; Stulp et al. 2016; Fieder & Huber 2022), the U.K. (Nettle & Pollet 2008), Norway (Lappegård & Rønsen 2013), Sweden (Fieder & Huber 2007; Goodman & Koupil 2010; Kolk & Barclay 2021; Kolk 2022), and Finland (Nisén et al. 2018). Data from Sweden show that even unexpected wealth in the form of winning the lottery is associated with increased fertility for men (Cesarini et al. 2023). Fieder and Huber (2012) found that having power in the workforce such as being in a supervisory position or in a position to hire and fire, which is likely correlated with income, also predicts a higher number of children in men.

This positive relationship exists mostly because higher-income men are more likely than lower-income men to be married. Fieder and Huber (2022) found a positive association between male income and ever being married in U.S. data from the Wisconsin Longitudinal Study, a long-term study of a random sample of men and women who were born between 1937 and 1940 and who graduated from Wisconsin high schools in 1957. They found that that for men income predicted 18% of the variance of ever being married. These results are in line with Hopcroft (2021) who showed using U.S. data that high-income men are more likely to marry, less likely to divorce, and more likely to remarry after divorce. Fieder and Huber (2022) also found that while being married explains about 73% of a man's number of children, male income itself explains only about 1% of the variation in the number of children. Thus, the positive association of male income with ever being married is much stronger than the association with the number of children in terms of variance explained.

The importance of income as a determining factor in marriage for men has been increasing during the last few decades, according to Fieder and Huber (2023). On the basis of U.S. Census data from 1940 to 2019, analyzed in 10-year steps, they found that the variance of ever being married explained by income in men aged 46–55 years increased from 2.5% in 1940 to around 20% in 2019. This suggests that women in the U.S. place greater importance on the income of a potential mate today than they did in 1940 (Fieder & Huber 2023).

For both men and women, there are fewer studies of the relationship between wealth or assets and fertility than of the relationship between income and fertility. Studies from the U.S. suggest that wealth is less of an important predictor of fertility than income for men and women. For example, Stulp et al. (2016) using wealth (defined including the worth of their home, cash savings, stock and bond portfolios, estate, business, and automobile assets, along with retirement and other saving plans minus debt accumulated by the

Status and fertility in post-transition Europe and America   83

time respondents were 47–56 years old) was positively associated with lifetime reproductive success at age 45 for black men only. Stulp et al. (2016) also found that lagged wealth from the previous 2 and 3 years increased the probability of a first and second birth for white men only (independent of income) although there was a negative effect on the probability of a third birth. In women, they found a positive effect of net worth on lifetime reproductive success for white women only. These mixed results are echoed in other studies. For example, for the U.S., Hopcroft (2019) found no effect of personal wealth on fertility and mostly negative relationships between household wealth and fertility for men and women when personal income and family income were controlled, while Schneider (2011) found that asset ownership was positively associated with the transition to a first marriage for men and also for women up until the mid-thirties.

Income and fertility within couples

All these studies show a clear difference in the association of personal income with fertility for men and women, with more mixed effects of wealth or assets. Other research suggests that the positive association between income and fertility for men is because low-income men are more likely to be childless than high-income men (von Rueden et al. 2011; Fieder et al. 2011; Barthold et al. 2012; Hopcroft 2015, 2021). The opposite is true for women, as high-income women are more likely to be childless than low-income women (Abma & Martinez 2006; Frejka 2017; Fieder & Huber 2020; Verweij et al. 2021) although once again there is evidence that this is changing in Scandinavia (Kolk 2022).

Most childbearing takes place within the context of long-term partnerships or marriages. Given the opposite effects of income on the number of children for men and women, and because women are more likely to reduce the number of hours they work outside of the home when they have children, in couples, it is necessary to examine the effects of men's and women's income separately. When this is done, Fleisher and Rhodes (1979), Freedman and Thornton (1982), Weeden et al. (2006), and Huber et al. (2010) all found a positive relationship in the U.S. between husband's income and wife's number of children when education was controlled, while Butz and Ward (1979) and Hopcroft (2019) found evidence that husband's income was positively associated with fertility and wife's income was negatively associated with fertility while even without controlling for education. Using a 2014 probability sample of husbands and wives drawn from the U.S. population that collected full fertility histories from both men and women, Hopcroft (2022) found that for wives, their personal income was negatively associated with their number of biological children, while their spouse's income was positively associated with their number of biological children. The opposite was true for husbands. This was found with or without controls for education and was not a result of childlessness among lower-income men and

84 *Status and fertility in post-transition Europe and America*

higher-income women. For the 45–65 age group, an age when fertility for most men and women is completed and yet people are unlikely to be retired, with no controls for education, there was a positive relationship between a woman's husband's income and her number of children, and a positive relationship between a man's personal income and his number of children.

Thus there is evidence that in the U.S. for men personal income is positively associated with number of offspring, and for women it is their husband's income that is positively related to their number of children; this is not due to the greater prevalence of childlessness among low-income men and high-income women. These relationships may hold also in other developed societies. For example, Fieder and Huber (2020) found using census data that the husband's income was positively associated with the wife's fertility in Israel.

Evolutionary theory and low fertility in developed societies

While the positive relationship between status as measured by personal income and fertility for men in modern societies supports predictions of evolutionary theory, some have argued that the lowest of the low fertility rates and below-replacement fertility in many developed societies contradicts evolutionary theory (e.g., Vining 2011). If the populations of those countries where the population has the most access to resources are shrinking, and the populations of those countries where the population has the least access to resources are growing, how can that be compatible with evolutionary theory, which suggests that the access to resources is crucial for reproduction?

This ostensible contradiction arises because fertility rates are an aggregate product of a country, and evolutionary theory is a theory of individuals. Reproductive success is always relative to the breeding group, as fitness measures an individual's share in future gene pools – not absolute fertility (see also Turke 1990; Jones & Bird 2014). The breeding group for all humans is shaped by cultural and geographic factors such as marriage rules and national borders, and individuals compete with each other for social status, resources, and to find mates within their group (Alexander 1987, 1989; Irons 1998). Individuals also calibrate their number of children and invest in their offspring so they will be competitive within the group (Turke 1989, 1990; Irons 1998; Shenk et al. 2016). As Turke (1990) noted: "decisions about the distribution of parental resources ... depend on how others are distributing such resources." Thus we have the seemingly paradoxical relationship of the richest countries having much lower fertility than the poorest countries.

Such status and resource competition for self and offspring may limit individuals' absolute fitness, but will not necessarily limit their relative fitness in the group. Even in societies with extremely low fertility, outcomes for high-status individuals are adaptive if those individuals continue to have a greater share of the subsequent gene pools. In the U.S., Europe and East Asia there is evidence that men with high personal incomes continue to have higher fertility than others. In the U.S. there is also evidence that women with higher-income

Status and fertility in post-transition Europe and America   85

husbands have more children than those with lower income husbands. In Sweden, there is evidence that higher personal income (including benefits and transfers from the state) is associated with greater fertility for both men and women (Kolk 2022). This suggests that individual reproductive behavior in modern societies continues to be adaptive.

Possible genetic selection

Any evolutionary approach assumes that key human predispositions, such as for status-striving, have a genetic basis. A logical question is, then, how are the changes in the modern world exerting selection pressure on the relevant genes? Genes are clearly involved in education and income, both of which are important markers of social status in modern societies. We know that up to 50% of lifetime income is genetically/epigenetically heritable, although percentages differ substantially depending on the sample investigated. In the MIDUS twin sample (the Midlife in the USA survey including 340 monozygotic twins and 512 dizygotic twins), for instance, controlled for sex and age, the heritable differences among individuals are about 52% for yearly income, 38% for highest education level ever attained, and only 14% for whether someone is in a supervisory or leading position. These heritability estimates on the basis of the MIDUS sample are in line with estimates based on Finnish twins showing that about 40% of the variance of women's lifetime earnings and somewhat more than 50% of men's lifetime earnings are linked to genetic factors (Hyytinen et al. 2019). Several other studies on the heritability of income end up with comparable estimates (reviewed in Hyytinen et al. 2019).

The heritability of income is likely mediated by genetic associations with certain personality traits, most of all intelligence (Fieder & Huber, unpublished data). This view is supported by a recent study of Hill et al. (2019) who first discovered, in a genome-wide association study on the basis of ~286,000 U.K. biobank participants, 149 genetic loci associated with household income, which despite being not a precise description of individual income may be used as an estimate. By combining this study with data from "expression quantitative trait loci studies" (eQTL), Hill et al. (2019) then identified 24 genes associated with income, of which 18 are known being associated with intelligence, which is also substantially heritable (20%–50% depending on the measure; Plomin & von Stumm 2018). Hence, intelligence appears to be one "missing link" explaining at least to some extent the genetic heritability of income.

An investigation of surnames over centuries by Gregory Clark provides additional evidence that inherited abilities might be important for a person's social status. Clark (2014) investigated how long certain surnames persisted in the social strata of their origin using data available over generations from the U.S., Sweden, U.K., Japan, Korea, and India. The expectation was that over time, the frequency of all surnames in a population should show a regression to the mean. Although this expectation was met, that is,

86 *Status and fertility in post-transition Europe and America*

both surnames originating from the higher strata moved downward and the surnames originating in lower strata moved upward, this occurred much more slowly than expected and did not follow a random process. These data indicate that social stratification is more persistent than previously thought, which may be because of the intergenerational transmission of social status, inherited genetic characteristics of individuals in different strata, or both.

There are also genetic correlates of educational outcomes, and as we have seen the level of education is often negatively associated with the number of children for both men and women, suggesting that there may be selection against genes associated with education. Genetic predispositions are often measured using polygenic scores. These measure the sum of the often very small effects on phenotype of several different genetic variants (single nucleotide polymorphisms or SNPS) in an individual's genotype. The effects of each genetic variant or SNPS themselves is usually estimated by genome-wide association studies. The resulting polygenic score is a measure of an individual's genetic propensity for a certain phenotype. Using individual data that included polygenic scores for education, Beauchamp (2016) and Kong et al. (2017) found a negative relationship between the polygenic score for education and the number of children and concluded there was selection against genes for education.

However, the association between genes for education and fertility may not be straightforward and likely differs between men and women. Fieder and Huber (2022) have been able to show, in men but not in women, that the polygenic score for education has an indirect positive effect on reproduction via a positive interaction with the polygenic scores for wages. Thus, albeit the genetic predisposition for education per se is negatively associated with the number of children, the same predisposition is associated with higher income in men and hence higher fertility. Hence, a genetic predisposition for education is associated with increased fitness in those men who convert higher education into higher income, whereas level of education itself resulted in lower reproduction, likely as a result of a decreased fertility window due to the postponement of reproduction (Fieder & Huber 2022). This holds particularly true for women. In women, a comparison of the effects of the phenotype level of education and its genetic predisposition indicates that it is the level of education itself (and the time necessary to obtain it) rather than its genetic predisposition that interferes with reproduction.

It is true that the findings of a positive relationship between status and fertility particularly for men in contemporary societies indicate that a directional positive selection pressure on the genetic correlates of social status might still exist in men, as was the case in historical and prehistorical times. Yet it is difficult to draw conclusions about the nature of selective pressures. Particularly in women, the situation is very different today than it was in the past. Although women had and still have reproductive benefits from a

Status and fertility in post-transition Europe and America 87

preference for men of higher social status, in modern societies women also strive for their own social status by increasing their education and personal income. High income increases resource availability but at a cost of putting the women under reproductive stress in terms of a limited fertility window, and in most industrial societies it can be difficult to combine a career with childbearing. Thus, recently in women a negative directional selection pressure on the genetic correlates of social status may be in place, although current evidence from Sweden (Kolk 2022) suggests that this may change. Thus, it is by far too early to make any final conclusions.

To conclude, if status is defined as education, for both men and women education tends to be negatively associated with fertility in modern societies. Much of this is due to the postponement of fertility due to education, and the negative effect tends to be stronger for women than it is for men. Yet there are signs that this negative effect is changing. In recent cohorts in East Asia and the Nordic countries, the relationship between education and fertility for women has become flat, U-shaped, or even positive. In these countries the relationship between education and fertility for men in recent cohorts has become mostly positive.

Yet education in modern societies is more a prerequisite for income than anything else, and income is likely the better measure of the social and material resources that facilitate reproduction. If status is defined as personal income, there is a great deal of evidence that the association of a man's status with reproduction in modern societies is positive. Much of this relationship (but not all) exists because high-income men are more likely to marry or be selected as mates than low-income men, and as a result are less likely to be childless. For women in the U.S., while personal income tends to be negatively associated with fertility, if status is defined as husband's income, then the association of status with reproduction is still positive. In Sweden, where the state provides generous parental leave and child allowances, there is evidence for recent cohorts that women's own income is positively associated with fertility just as it is for men.

Thus even in modern societies characterized by the lowest of the low fertility at the aggregate level, there is evidence of a positive relationship between status and fertility at the individual level as predicted by evolutionary theory. Although the positive relationship between status and fertility in modern populations is much smaller and overall levels of fertility are much lower than in preindustrial populations, it is likely that modern fertility behavior continues to be adaptive. This suggests that modern societies are much less anomalous to preindustrial societies than once thought.

References

Abma, J. C., & Martinez, G. M. (2006). Childlessness among older women in the United States: Trends and profiles. *Journal of Marriage and Family*, 68, 1045–1056.

88 *Status and fertility in post-transition Europe and America*

Alexander, R. D. (1987) *The biology of moral systems.* Rutgers, NJ: Transaction Publishers.

Alexander, R. D. (1989) Evolution of the human psyche. In P. Mellars & C. B. Stringer (Eds.), *The Human Revolution: Behavioural and Biological Perspectives on the Origins of Modern Humans.* Princeton University Press, pp. 455–513.

Andersson, G., Rønsen, M., Knudsen, L. B., Lappegård, T., Neyer, G., Skrede, K., et al. (2009). Cohort fertility patterns in the Nordic countries. *Demographic Research,* 20(14), 313–352.

Barthold, J. A., Myrskylä, M. & Jones, O. R. (2012) Childlessness drives the sex difference in the association between income and reproductive success of modern Europeans. *Evolution and Human Behavior* 33(6), 628–638.

Beauchamp, J. P. (2016). Genetic evidence for natural selection in humans in the contemporary United States. *Proceedings of the National Academy of Sciences,* 113(28), 7774–7779.

Beaujouan, E., Brzozowska, Z., & Zeman, K. (2016). The limited effect of increasing educational attainment on childlessness trends in twentieth-century Europe, women born 1916–65. *Population Studies,* 70(3), 275–291.

Brzozowska, Z., Beaujouan, E., & Zeman, K. (2022). Is two still best? Change in parity-specific fertility across education in low-fertility countries. *Population Research and Policy Review,* 1–30.

Butz, W. P., and M. P. Ward. (1979). The emergence of countercyclical U.S. fertility. *American Economic Review* 69(3):318–28.

Cesarini, D., Lindqvist, E., Östling, R., & Terskaya, A. (2023). *Fortunate families? The effects of wealth on marriage and fertility (No. w31039).* National Bureau of Economic Research.

Clark, G. (2014). *The son also rises.* Princeton, NJ: Princeton University Press. ISBN-10: 0691168377.

Fieder, M. & Huber, S. (2007) The effects of sex and childlessness on the association between status and reproductive output in modern society. *Evolution and Human Behavior* 28, 392–398.

Fieder, M., S. Huber, and F. L. Bookstein. (2011). Socioeconomic status, marital status and childlessness in men and women: An analysis of census data from six countries. *Journal of Biosocial Science* 43(5):619–35. doi:10.1017/S002193201100023X.

Fieder, M., & Huber, S. (2012). An evolutionary account of status, power, and career in modern societies. *Human Nature,* 23, 191–207.

Fieder, M., & Huber, S. (2020). Effects of wife's and husband's income on wife's reproduction: An evolutionary perspective on human mating. *Biodemography and Social Biology,* 65(1), 31–40.

Fieder, M., & Huber, S. (2022). Contemporary selection pressures in modern societies? Which factors best explain variance in human reproduction and mating? *Evolution and Human Behavior,* 43(1), 16–25.

Fieder, M., & Huber, S. (2023). Increasing pressure on US men for income in order to find a spouse. *Biodemography and Social Biology,* 68:2-3, 1–19.

Fleisher, B. M., and G. Rhodes. (1979). Fertility, women's wage rates, and labor supply. *American Economic Review* 69(1):14–24.

Freedman, D. S., and A. Thornton. (1982). Income and fertility: The elusive relationship. *Demography* 19(1):65–78.

Status and fertility in post-transition Europe and America 89

Frejka, T. (2017). Childlessness in the United States. In M. Kreyenfeld & D. Konietzka (Eds), *Childlessness in Europe: Contexts, causes, and consequences* (pp. 159–179). Cham: Springer Nature.

Goodman, A., & Koupil, I. (2010). The effect of school performance upon marriage and long-term reproductive success in 10,000 Swedish males and females born 1915–1929. *Evolution and Human Behavior, 31*(6), 425–435.

Guzzo, K. B., & Hayford, S. R. (2020). Pathways to parenthood in social and family contexts: Decade in review. *Journal of Marriage and Family, 82*(1), 117–144.

Hill, W. D., Davies, N. M., Ritchie, S. J., Skene, N. G., Bryois, J., Bell, S., ... & Deary, I. J. (2019). Genome-wide analysis identifies molecular systems and 149 genetic loci associated with income. *Nature Communications, 10*(1), 5741.

Hopcroft, R. L. (2006) Sex, status and reproductive success in the contemporary U.S. *Evolution and Human Behavior* 27, 104–120.

Hopcroft, R. L. (2015) Sex differences in the relationship between status and number of offspring in the contemporary U.S. *Evolution and Human Behavior* 36(2), 146–151.

Hopcroft, R. L. (2019). Sex differences in the association of family and personal income and wealth with fertility in the United States. *Human Nature* 30:477–95.

Hopcroft, R. L. (2021). High income men have high value as long-term mates in the US: Personal income and the probability of marriage, divorce, and childbearing in the US. *Evolution and Human Behavior* 42:409–17.

Hopcroft, R. L. (2022). Husband's income, wife's income, and number of biological children in the US. *Biodemography and Social Biology, 67*(1), 71–83.

Huber, S., F. L. Bookstein, and M. Fieder. (2010). Socioeconomic status, education, and reproduction in modern women: An evolutionary perspective. *American Journal of Human Biology* 22 (5):578–87.

Hudde, A., & Engelhardt, H. (2023). Family inequality. *Demographic Research, 48*, 549–590.

Hyytinen, A., Ilmakunnas, P., Johansson, E., & Toivanen, O. (2019). Heritability of lifetime earnings. *Journal of Economic Inequality, 17*, 319–335.

Irons, W. (1998) Adaptively relevant environments versus the environment of evolutionary adaptedness. *Evolutionary Anthropology* 6(6), 194–204.

Jalovaara, M., Neyer, G., Andersson, G., Dahlberg, J., Dommermuth, L., Fallesen, P., & Lappegård, T. (2019). Education, gender, and cohort fertility in the Nordic countries. *European Journal of Population, 35*(3), 563–586.

Jones, J. H. & Bird, R. B. (2014) The marginal valuation of fertility. *Evolution and Human Behavior* 35(1), 65–71.

Kaptijn, R., Thomese, F., van Tilburga, T. G., Liefbroera, A. C. & Deeg, D. J. H. (2010) Low fertility in contemporary humans and the mate value of their children: sex-specific effects on social status indicators. *Evolution and Human Behavior* 31, 59–68.

Kolk, M. (2022). The relationship between life-course accumulated income and childbearing of Swedish men and women born 1940–70. *Population Studies*.

Kolk, M., and K. Barclay. (2021). Do income and marriage mediate the relationship between cognitive ability and fertility? Data from Swedish taxation and conscriptions registers for men born 1951– 1967. *Intelligence* 84:101514.

Kong, A., Frigge, M. L., Thorleifsson, G., Stefansson, H., Young, A. I., Zink, F., ... & Stefansson, K. (2017). Selection against variants in the genome associated with

90 *Status and fertility in post-transition Europe and America*

educational attainment. *Proceedings of the National Academy of Sciences*, 114(5), E727–E732.

Kravdal, Ø., & Rindfuss, R. R. (2008). Changing relationships between education and fertility: A study of women and men born 1940 to 1964. *American Sociological Review*, 73(5), 854–873.

Lappegård, T. & Rønsen, M. (2013) Socioeconomic differences in multipartner fertility among Norwegian men. *Demography* 50, 1135–1153.

Nettle, D. & Pollet, T. V. (2008) Natural selection on male wealth in humans. *American Naturalist* 172(5), 658–666.

Nisén, J., Klüsener, S., Dahlberg, J., Dommermuth, L., Jasilioniene, A., Kreyenfeld, M., ... & Myrskylä, M. (2021). Educational differences in cohort fertility across sub-national regions in Europe. *European Journal of Population*, 37, 263–295.

Nisén, J., Martikainen, P., Kaprio, J. & Silventoinen, K. (2013) Educational differences in completed fertility: A behavioral genetic study of Finnish male and female twins. *Demography* 50(4), 1399–1420.

Nisén, J., P. Martikainen, M. Myrskylä, and K. Silventoinen. 2018. Education, other socioeconomic characteristics across the life course, and fertility among Finnish men. *European Journal of Population* 34 (3):337–66.

Plomin, R., & Von Stumm, S. (2018). The new genetics of intelligence. *Nature Reviews Genetics*, 19(3), 148–159.

Schneider, D. (2011). Wealth and the marital divide. *American Journal of Sociology* 117(2):627–67.

Shenk, M. K., Kaplan, H. S. & Hooper, P. L. (2016) Status competition, inequality, and fertility: Implications for the demographic transition. *Philosophical Transactions of the Royal Society* Series B 371, 20150150.

Stulp, G., R. Sear, S. B. Schaffnit, M. C. Mills, and L. Barrett. (2016). The reproductive ecology of industrial societies part II the association between wealth and fertility. *Human Nature* 27 (4):445–70.

Turke, P. W. (1989) Evolution and the demand for children. *Population and Development Review* 15(1), 61–90.

Turke, P. W. (1990) Which humans behave adaptively, and why does it matter? *Ethology and Sociobiology* 11, 305–339.

U.S. Census. (2018). Current Population Survey 2018. www.census.gov/data/tables/2018/demo/ fertility/women-fertility.html#par_list_61. Table 4.

Van Bavel, J., Klesment, M., Beaujouan, E., Brzozowska, Z., Puur, A., Reher, D., et al. (2018). Seeding the gender revolution: Women's education and cohort fertility among the baby boom generations. *Population Studies*, 72(3), 283–304.

Verweij, R. M., Stulp, G., Snieder, H., & Mills, M. C. (2021). Explaining the associations of education and occupation with childlessness: The role of desires and expectations to remain childless. *Population Review*, 60(2), 166–194.

Vining, D. R. Jr (2011) Commentary. Sociobiology's relevance to modern society: commentary on two articles published here. *Evolution and Human Behavior* 32, 364–367.

Von Rueden, C., Gurven, M., & Kaplan, H. (2011). Why do men seek status? Fitness payoffs to dominance and prestige. *Proceedings of the Royal Society B: Biological Sciences*, 278(1715), 2223–2232.

Weeden, J., M. J. Abrams, M. C. Green, and J. Sabini. (2006). Do high status people really have fewer children? Education, income, and fertility in the contemporary U.S. *Human Nature* 17:377–92.

Wood, J., Marynissen, L., Nisén, J., Fallesen, P., Neels, K., Trimarchi, A., ... & Martikainen, P. (2021). Regional variation in women's education-fertility nexus in Northern and Western Europe. MPIDR Working Papers, Max Planck Institute for Demographic Research, Rostock, Germany.

9 Additional factors influencing status and fertility

As we saw in Chapter 3, a common way that status is attained across human societies is through cultural activities, including rituals and other activities associated with religion. Some sort of religion or set of spiritual beliefs is important in all preindustrial societies, and most religions or spiritual beliefs include precepts regarding the family. Another constant we saw in many human societies, particularly stratified societies, are strict rules of endogamy or homogamy – people marrying other people of the same group or class. These rules are frequently associated with religious precepts. For these reasons it is not surprising that religion, homogamy, and social status are intertwined and have implications for fertility in most societies, including modern societies.

Religion

Of the factors influencing both social status and fertility, religion is probably the most important. Contrary to social status, which provides reproductive advantages more to men than to women, in contemporary societies religion has a similar pro-fertility effect in both men and women. Religion increases reproductive output irrespective of sex and social status. In both men and women in the U.S., extrinsic religiosity in terms of attendance of religious services, for instance, explains about 2% of the variance in the lifetime number of children (data from Wisconsin Longitudinal Study, Fieder & Huber 2022).

We know that education, income, and religiosity have at least in part a genetic basis (as shown by twin studies as well as GWA studies; Day et al. 2018, Koenig et al. 2005). Consequently, if those traits have a pro-fertility effect, the alleles associated with one or both traits (in the case of pleiotropy) will eventually spread in the population. It is thus reasonable to assume that genes associated with status-seeking behavior and religiosity may have been to some extent under selection in the more recent evolution of our species (Norenzayan 2013; Huber & Fieder 2018; Fieder & Huber 2021a). In addition, they possibly could be more intertwined than previously thought.

DOI: 10.4324/9781003463320-9

Evidence for a potential genetic interrelation between status-seeking and religiosity is provided by the genetic association of education and religiosity, as for individuals level of education is to some extent predicted by the individual's polygenic score for religious participation and vice versa, indicating some overlapping genetic regions associated with religious participation and educational attainment (Fieder & Huber 2022). At a first glance, these results seem surprising as being highly educated is often negatively associated with religious behavior in that more highly educated people are often less likely to express religious beliefs or attend religious services (Meisenberg et al. 2012). Nonetheless, the genetic association still seems reasonable if the cognitive, imaginary, and intellectual aspects of religion are considered. Being religious requires to some extent learning the rules, the rituals, and the habits of religion (Atran & Henrich 2010; Norenzayan 2013) and this can be regarded as similar to the learning and activities involved in formal education.

The universality of some sort of religious behavior in all cultures also suggests that a tendency toward religiosity is a product of evolution. By and large, theories of the evolution of religiosity are of two types – "by-product" and "adaptation" theories (Sanderson 2018). "By-product" theories view religiosity as a by-product of traits evolved for some other purpose. For example, Boyer (2008) suggests that religious concepts and norms are parasitic upon standard cognitive systems that evolved outside of religion, such as agency-detection, moral intuition, coalitional psychology, and contagion-avoidance. "Adaptationist" theories view religiosity as an adaptive trait that helped our ancestors survive and reproduce in the past. For example, Alcorta and Sosis (2005) argue that engagement in religious rituals and other practices are a form of costly signaling that demonstrate group commitment and so enhance group cooperation, and this in turn provides benefits for the individual.

It is possible that religiosity evolved initially as a by-product of our cognitive evolution, but later on direct selection fostered the further evolution of religiosity. It may be that the evolution of religiosity took place during the evolution of our cognition system, presumably during the evolution of the skill of "mentalizing." Mentalizing is the ability to ascribe mental states to other humans, often called "theory of mind." At some point in human evolution this ability emerged and it facilitated individual understanding and prediction of the mental states of others. This ability also facilitated the anthropomorphizing of animals, plants, and even inanimate objects, giving them human-like minds with intentions and beliefs. This may have in turn promoted belief in small gods and spirits; it may also have facilitated humans imagining what would happen to an individual after death (reviewed in Norenzayan et al. 2016, Norenzayan 2013). Importantly, the cognitive capabilities associated with the ability to put oneself in another person's position may also have promoted the emergence of more complex rules of cooperation and pro-sociality. The sense that someone else feels and suffers the

94   *Factors influencing status and fertility*

same way as self may encourage people not to harm others but to act pro-socially. This may also have encouraged the development of moral systems and religious sentiments. Another effect of the evolution of the ability to mentalize is the ability to understand social causalities such as "if I act in a certain manner, this person is likely to react in such and such a way." This insight enabled individuals to develop strategies to gain social status within a group. The ability to recognize social causalities may have also promoted the ability to recognize causalities such as the effects of the seasonality of nature. Recognizing causalities may also have helped individuals conceive of supernatural creators or gods. Pro-social and moral behaviors associated with religious sentiments likely provided individual reproductive benefits, as those who acted pro-socially and helped others were likely in turn to receive more help from others. These pro-social individuals would likely have had more access to resources and may also have had greater social status, which would have been a benefit in reproduction. Such reproductive benefits would have facilitated the evolution of a predisposition toward moral and religious behaviors and beliefs.

Tribal populations usually do not have moralizing big gods (see below) but rather many "small gods" and spirits. In contrast to big gods, these small gods and spirits do not often interfere with everyday life. In history, the emergence of complex religions and moral codes and the idea of big gods only developed once humans were living in agrarian societies in large social groups. The development of the idea of "big gods" who punish someone who behaves badly may have helped to stabilize newly emerging, larger social groups. As the first states emerged, individuals of many different backgrounds would have gathered in larger agglomerations. Their differences very likely led to conflicts among the different groups. A common religion with a big god who would punish transgressions would have helped to overcome these conflicts. This may have been essential, as in the very earliest states laws were often not prescribed in detail nor fully enforced. Accordingly, big gods who are almighty and "see everything" may have been very important in ensuring cooperation and fostering pro-sociality among different and unrelated individuals in large-scale social groups. Big gods and/or complex religions would have also helped ensure cooperation despite the growing social inequalities (reviewed in Norenzayan et al. 2016, Norenzayan 2013). As we saw in Chapter 3, in medieval Habsburg and the Holy Roman Empire, the emperor did not get his authority just by mundane power but by the eternal entity, starting with the coronation of Charlemagne by Pope Leo III on December 25, 800, in Rome. While this tradition was modified over the centuries, the principal tradition of the Holy Roman emperor remained for 1,000 years until the Habsburg emperor Franz II.

If religiosity evolved because it had adaptive benefits for individuals, we would expect that religious individuals in most societies would have more offspring. Indeed, as noted previously, in contemporary societies the evidence is that religious individuals do have more children. The pro-fertility effects of religious affiliation as compared to nonaffiliation as well as the pro-fertility effects of religious intensity (both extrinsic such as the attendance of religious services as well as intrinsic such as praying and spirituality) are so strong that modern-day religious groups are expected to grow merely due to the fertility of their adherents (Hackett et al. 2015). The Mormons are an example, as typical Mormon families usually are larger on average than other U.S. families (Heaton 1986). Moreover, the more deeply individuals are committed to their religion (measured for instance by church attendance, frequency of praying, self-estimate of spirituality), the higher their average number of children compared to average family size of religious noncommitted individuals (Blume 2009; Fieder & Huber 2016).

Endogamy and homogamy

In nearly all religions there are rules of in-group cooperation. These are rules to foster cooperation between religious peers and to support them. On the downside, these rules may also mean less cooperation outside the group. This boundary between in-group and out-group is reflected by the fact that in history there have been frequent conflicts at the borders of religions and between adherents of different religious traditions. In addition to rules of in-group cooperation, rules of in-group marriage are also common in religion, ensuring that only individuals of the same religious community marry each other. Examples include in the Hebrew bible, Deuteronomy 7:3: "Do not take wives or husbands from among them (the disbelieving); do not give your daughters to their sons or take their daughters for your sons"; the Quran 2:221: "And do not marry polytheistic women until they believe," or the Quran 60:10: "And hold not to marriage bonds with disbelieving women." Such rules of religious in-group marriage or endogamy are another mechanism by which religions increase individual reproductive success (Whitmeyer 1997; Fox 2015), as there is evidence that religious in-group marriage is positively associated with reproductive success. With some exceptions (for instance in countries such as Brazil with newly emerging syncretic religions), spouses who are married within their own religious faith have on average more children and also remain childless less frequently than couples marrying outside their own religious group (Fieder & Huber 2016). The main reason for this finding may be that husbands and wives who share a religion also share a better understanding of each other and hence experience greater marital harmony.

In-group preferences also have in part a genetic basis (from ~19% to 46%, depending on the trait, see Fieder & Huber 2021b) although only religious in-group preference and religious homogamy, but not ethnic in-group preferences, have reproductive benefits (Fox 2015; Fieder & Huber 2021b). On an ultimate level, religious homogamy may thus additionally help the spread of alleles associated with religion in the population. Even though homogamy per se does not alter gene frequencies, the frequency of alleles

96 Factors influencing status and fertility

for which spouses are homogamous will eventually spread in the population if homogamous couples have a higher number of offspring (Relethford 2012). Furthermore, due to homogamy, the percentage of the genome that each individual may transfer to the next generation may exceed the statistical mean of 50% (Rushton 1989).

Generally, homogamy on a certain trait may hold variability low and thus may accelerate biological adaption (Fox 2015), but this comes at a price (as does everything in biology). Ethnic in-group preference, for instance, may lead to more in-group marriages, which may also mean more marriages within kin networks. This view is supported by a recent study, showing that more and longer runs of homozygosity (a genetic indicator for a history of inbreeding in a population) are associated with ethnic in-group preferences (data from the U.S., Australia; Fieder et al. 2021), which may lead to the well-known problems associated with inbreeding (Clark et al. 2019; Ceballos et al. 2018). Hence, a balance between homogamy (making variability not too high) and heterogamy (enabling variability) may have been a genetically optimal strategy (Fox 2015).

Homogamy and kin marriages, however, have consequences beyond reproductive benefits and inbreeding costs. In-group and kin marriage, in that they lead to more offspring and more relatives, are also associated with social status. As documented impressively by Napoleon Chagnon and the Yanomami (see Chapter 4), simply having more relatives can be a source of power. The more kin to provide support in times of conflict that a village leader has, the more powerful he is. Reproductive success may thus lead to social status simply by numbers.

Furthermore, kin marriage can help keep wealth within families and larger kin networks. In the case of family-owned assets and property, for instance, future wealth will concentrate in the kin network whenever the progeny of property-owning siblings marry each other. In the case of land ownership, this marriage strategy not only keeps wealth in families but also avoids the fragmentation of land. Generally, in-group marriage may have two economic rationales: (1) the aim to consolidate and preserve family assets and property, and (2) the aim to reduce the matrimonial expenditures involved in unions (reviewed in Salem & Shah 2019). These economic rationales are likely to be most salient for those groups with the most assets and property, and so suggest that in-group marriage will be most common among wealthier groups. Although both economic rationales have been reported from societies where kin marriage is common, not many quantitative studies have been conducted to evaluate the evidence. One study on representative Egypt data shows that men originating from land-owning households and also grooms from agriculturally more wealthy origins indeed tend to marry kin (first-order cousins) more frequently than others (Salem & Shah 2019). Moreover, women who married relatives reported lower bride's side matrimonial expenditures (Salem & Shah 2019). These findings support the view that "in-group marriages" may confer economic advantages and that families in a better economic position have the most reason to choose to keep wealth among relatives.

As an example, royalty and associated nobility in Europe have been keeping social status, power, and wealth within families for centuries in part due to their marriage practices. While European empires did fight each other, European royalty also commonly married within kin networks. These in-group marriage patterns, however, also had negative health consequences as has been impressively documented by the hemophilia of Alexei Nikolaevich, tsarevich of Russia, who was the only son of the last tsar of Russia Nikolaus II. The tsarevich's hemophilia can be traced back to his grand-grandmother Queen Victoria of England who was a carrier of the gene for hemophilia. Also the iconic "Habsburg chin" formed by inbreeding is a visible effect of kin marriages (Vilas et al. 2019). Indeed, almost all of Europe's existing royalty are relatives to some extent. These royal individuals wove a noble "homogamy network" over whole Europe that helped ensure power, status, and wealth over the centuries. The House of Welf from the 9th century, for instance, is represented in almost all European dynasties.

Are there selective forces that may have fostered predispositions toward homogamy and endogamy during our evolution? What we know is that in-group cohesion would have been very important during our lives in small-scale societies, where we may have lived in small groups of not much more than approximately 150 individuals (Dunbar 1993). Although the so-called Dunbar's number of 150 has been frequently criticized, it still provides a rather reasonable assumption of group size based on the ratio of neo-cortex size and group size in primates. Life in such small groups likely posed a fundamental problem. In order to keep resources within a group, in-group marriages and thus homogamy are advantageous. At the same time, how-ever, as discussed previously, too many in-group marriages will lead to higher rates of inbreeding and thus the detrimental genetical effects associated with inbreeding (Clark et al. 2019; Ceballos et al. 2018; Fieder et al. 2021). Out-group marriages as a means to avoid inbreeding, however, also may pose problems as contacts among different groups may be dangerous and even lethal. This holds true particularly for men as indicated by genetic data and the frequently found remains of massacres (Schahbasi et al. 2021). The evo-lution that resulted because of these problems of group living likely shaped our attitudes toward in-group versus out-group and may have shaped ten-dencies toward homogamy versus exogamy.

Another hint that tendencies toward homogamy are evolved is the evi-dence that homogamy has in part a genetic basis. We know that both in-group preferences and the attitude to homogamy have a genetic basis (from ~20% to 50%, depending on the trait investigated, Fieder & Huber 2021b). This holds true, however, only for the "established" forms of homogamy such as ethnic and religious homogamy. The rather "new form of homogamy," educational homogamy, only has an almost negligible heritable component – lower than 5% (in preparation).

98 *Factors influencing status and fertility*

In preindustrial societies, kin marriage and homogamy have been common – often in the form of cross-cousin marriage (Fox 2015). Such practices were almost always based on tribal structure, ethnicity, and religion, and enforced by cultural and religious rules. In modern societies, however, a new form of homogamy has emerged: homogamy based on education. In the last 50 years or so, educational homogamy has become more and more important. Particularly, the higher educated tend to marry within their own social strata (Smits 2003; Huber & Fieder 2011; Huber & Fieder 2016). Hence, in modern societies, one of the most important prerequisites for social status is one of the most important criteria for mate selection.

In modern societies where more individuals are highly educated, marriages across different educational levels have become increasingly less frequent. U.S. census data from 1960, for instance, show that among male university graduates, about 67% married "down" (i.e., married women of lower educational attainment), whereas in the census of 2015, this percentage was less than half, so that only 32% of the male university graduates married "down." The main reason for this shift is that today more university graduate women are on the marriage market: university graduate women increased from 6.2% in 1960 to 32% in 2015, whereas in men, university graduates increased from 8.3% in 1960 to 29.3% in 2015. Thus, a male bias in university graduates in 1960 shifted to a female bias in 2015. In addition, the proportion of university graduates increased generally. As a consequence, university graduates now have a higher chance to find a mate among others like themselves than they did in 1960. So, university graduates have become more like a "tribe of their own." Educational homogamy may thus be a modern form of homogamy by social status as was the case among the nobles, rich farmers, and the like, who did not marry beneath their status. Today it means not to marry beneath your level of education.

While education can be viewed as a status indicator itself, as we noted in Chapter 8, it is likely more of a prerequisite of social status in modern societies. Nonetheless, educational homogamy may lead to a situation where education is much more concentrated at the top of the social hierarchy. This is a development that has detrimental social consequences of greater inequality and even less permeable societies (Kalmijn 1998; Kalmijn & Flap 2001; Mijs & Roe 2021). It may be that a certain proportion of the political polarization that we currently experience may be a result of the increasing encapsulation of the different educational strata, which may increase partisanship (Brown & Enos 2021).

As is the case with religious homogamy, educational homogamy has reproductive consequences. On the basis of the U.S. Census from 1980 ($n = 670,631$ married U.S. couples, only married once), Huber & Fieder (2011) showed that the proportion of childless individuals was lowest among women who were married to a husband of the same educational level. This effect of educational homogamy on childlessness was particularly pronounced among both the lowest and the highest educated women. Educational homogamy

Factors influencing status and fertility 99

was also associated with a younger age at first marriage. It did not, however, predict the number of children (Huber & Fieder 2011) as the mean number of children decreased with increasing educational level attained. As noted previously, this finding can be mostly attributed to the postponing of reproduction due to education. A high prevalence of educational homogamy is not only found in the U.S. but in an analysis of worldwide census data from 41 different countries (in total 2,179,736 married women; Huber & Fieder 2016). In other countries, however, it was a combination of moderate female hypergamy (meaning marrying a man higher in education) and homogamy that reduced the odds of childlessness. Again, the number of children was not associated with educational homogamy.

In addition to the increasing trend toward educational homogamy, however, female hypogamy (i.e., where the wife has more years of education than their husband) is increasing. In industrial societies, as more women finish a higher level of education, among the higher educated the sex ratio has changed from male bias to female bias, generating an education-specific mating squeeze (van Bavel 2012). Accordingly, Esteve et al. (2016) showed that among individuals aged between 25 and 29 years, in 139 countries, representing ~86% of the worldwide population, a higher ratio of women than men completed post-secondary education. The authors further expect that in 2050, in nearly every country in the world, a higher proportion of women will be better educated than men (Esteve et al. 2016).

This educational sex ratio reversal has and will have profound consequences for the mating market, patterns of assortative mating, marriage outcomes in terms of dissolution and divorce, and also for fertility and particularly for childlessness. The percentage of hypogamous couples, for instance, will increase, whereas that of the traditional hypergamous marriages will decrease. It is known from studies of European data (van Bavel 2012) that in families in which the woman is more highly educated than her spouse, the woman also is likely to provide the major source of income in the family. As regards marriage stability, family hypogamy and a higher income of women compared to men in couples leads to higher divorce rates in older but not younger U.S. cohorts (Schwartz & Gonalons-Pons 2016). However, given that education is positively associated with income and lower male income is associated with an increased risk of childlessness and an increased risk of divorce (Hopcroft 2006, 2015; Fieder et al. 2011; Fieder & Huber 2022), it is likely that trends toward educational hypogamy will promote an additional drop in fertility in almost all countries.

The case of Sweden demonstrates a somewhat different possible outcome. In the past 50 years Sweden has seen the development of an extensive welfare state including income substitution during parental leave (80%–90% of income pre childbirth) and generous child allowances. As a result, the most recent cohorts of women in Sweden have seen the reversal of the negative relationship between income (measured to include benefits and transfers) and

100 *Factors influencing status and fertility*

fertility for women and the emergence of a positive relationship between income and fertility for women as well as men (Kolk 2022).

Thus in this chapter we have seen that religiosity has a genetic basis and is likely a product of evolution. Religiosity was intertwined with social status in historical societies and so likely was also intertwined with reproductive success in the past. In the contemporary world, there is evidence that religious affiliation and behavior continue to be linked with reproductive advantage. Religion also promotes homogamy or in-group marriage, and there is evidence that this also has a positive effect on fertility. Modern societies also have extensive homogamy based on education, and while this does not have a positive effect on the number of children, it does help prevent childlessness.

References

Alcorta, C. S., & Sosis, R. (2005). Ritual, emotion, and sacred symbols. *Human Nature*, 16(4), 323–359.

Atran, S., & Henrich, J. (2010). The evolution of religion: How cognitive by-products, adaptive learning heuristics, ritual displays, and group competition generate deep commitments to prosocial religions. *Biological Theory*, 5, 18–30.

Blume, M. (2009). The reproductive benefits of religious affiliation. In E. Voland & W. Schiefenhövel (Eds), *The biological evolution of religious mind and behavior* (pp. 117–126). Heidelberg: Springer Science.

Boyer, P. (2008). *Religion explained*. New York: Random House.

Brown, J. R., & Enos, R. D. (2021). The measurement of partisan sorting for 180 million voters. *Nature Human Behaviour*, 5(8), 998–1008.

Ceballos, F. C., Joshi, P. K., Clark, D. W., Ramsay, M., & Wilson, J. F. (2018). Runs of homozygosity: Windows into population history and trait architecture. *Nature Reviews Genetics*, 19(4), 220–234.

Clark, D. W., Okada, Y., Moore, K. H., Mason, D., Pirastu, N., Gandin, I., & Deelen, P. (2019). Associations of autozygosity with a broad range of human phenotypes. *Nature Communications*, 10(1), 1–17.

Day, F. R., Ong, K. K., & Perry, J. R. (2018). Elucidating the genetic basis of social interaction and isolation. *Nature Communications*, 9(1), 2457.

Dunbar, R. I. (1993). Coevolution of neocortical size, group size and language in humans. *Behavioral and Brain Sciences*, 16(4), 681–694.

Esteve, A., Schwartz, C. R., van Bavel, J., Permanyer, I., Klesment, M., & Garcia, J. (2016). The end of hypergamy: Global trends and implications. *Population and Development Review*, 42(4), 615.

Fieder, M., & Huber, S. (2016). The association between religious homogamy and reproduction. *Proceedings of the Royal Society B: Biological Sciences*, 283(1834), 20160294.

Fieder, M., & Huber, S. (2021a). The evolutionary biology of religious behavior. *Interdisciplinary Journal for Religion and Transformation in Contemporary Society*, 7(1), 303–334.

Fieder, M., & Huber, S. (2021b). Fertility outcomes, heritability and genomic associations of in-group preference and in-group marriage. *Twin Research and Human Genetics*, 24(5), 264–272.

Fieder, M., & Huber, S. (2022). Contemporary selection pressures in modern societies? Which factors best explain variance in human reproduction and mating? *Evolution and Human Behavior*, 43(1), 16–25.

Fieder, M., Huber, S., & Bookstein, F. L. (2011). Socioeconomic status, marital status and childlessness in men and women: An analysis of census data from six countries. *Journal of Biosocial Science*, 43(5), 619–635.

Fieder, M., Mitchell, B. L., Gordon, S., Huber, S., & Martin, N. G. (2021). Ethnic identity and genome wide runs of homozygosity. *Behavior Genetics*, 51, 405–413.

Fox, R. (2015). Marry in or die out: Optimal inbreeding and the meaning of mediogamy. In A. Turner, J. H. Machalek, & R. Maryanskipp (Eds), *Handbook on evolution and society* (pp. 350–382). London: Routledge.

Hackett, C., Connor, P. Stonawski, M., Skirbekk, V., Potančoková, M., & Abel, G. (2015). The future of world religions: Population growth projections for 2010–2050. Pew Research Center www.pewforum.org/2015/04/02/religious-projections-2010-2050/ Last access November 21, 2023.

Heaton, T. B. (1986). How does religion influence fertility? The case of Mormons. *Journal for the Scientific Study of Religion*, 25(2), 248–258.

Hopcroft, R. L. (2006). Sex, status, and reproductive success in the contemporary United States. *Evolution and Human Behavior*, 27(2), 104–120.

Hopcroft, R. L. (2015). Sex differences in the relationship between status and number of offspring in the contemporary US. *Evolution and Human Behavior*, 36(2), 146–151.

Huber, S., & Fieder, M. (2011). Educational homogamy lowers the odds of reproductive failure. *PLoS One*, 6(7), e22330.

Huber, S., & Fieder, M. (2016). Worldwide census data reveal prevalence of educational homogamy and its effect on childlessness. *Frontiers in Sociology*, 1, 10.

Huber, S., & Fieder, M. (2018). Mutual compensation of the effects of religious and ethnic homogamy on reproduction. *American Journal of Human Biology*, 30(1), e23064.

Kalmijn, M. (1998). Intermarriage and homogamy: Causes, patterns, trends. *Annual Review of Sociology*, 24(1), 395–421.

Kalmijn, M., & Flap, H. (2001). Assortative meeting and mating: Unintended consequences of organized settings for partner choices. *Social Forces*, 79(4), 1289–1312.

Koenig, L. B., McGue, M., Krueger, R. F., & Bouchard Jr, T. J. (2005). Genetic and environmental influences on religiousness: Findings for retrospective and current religiousness ratings. *Journal of Personality*, 73(2), 471–488.

Kolk, M. (2022). The relationship between life-course accumulated income and childbearing of Swedish men and women born 1940–70. *Population Studies*, 1–19.

Meisenberg, G., Rindermann, H., Patel, H., & Woodley, M. A. (2012). Is it smart to believe in God? The relationship of religiosity with education and intelligence. *Temas em Psicologia*, 20(1), 101–121.

Mijs, J. J., & Roe, E. L. (2021). Is America coming apart? Socioeconomic segregation in neighborhoods, schools, workplaces, and social networks, 1970–2020. *Sociology Compass*, 15(6), e12884.

Norenzayan, A. (2013). *Big gods: How religion transformed cooperation and conflict*. Princeton, NJ: Princeton University Press. ISBN-10: 0691151210.

Norenzayan, A., Shariff, A. F., Gervais, W. M., Willard, A. K., McNamara, R. A., Slingerland, E., & Henrich, J. (2016). The cultural evolution of prosocial religions. *Behavioral and Brain Sciences*, 39, e1.

102 *Factors influencing status and fertility*

Relethford, J. H. (2012). *Human population genetics*. New York: Wiley.

Rushton, J. P. (1989). Genetic similarity, human altruism, and group selection. *Behavioral and Brain Sciences*, 12(3), 503–518.

Salem, R., & Shah, S. (2019). Economic rationales for kin marriage. *Demographic Research*, 41, 545–578.

Sanderson, S. K. (2018). From paganism to world transcendence: Religious attachment theory and the evolution of the world religions. In Rosemary L. Hopcroft (Ed.), *The Oxford Handbook of Evolution, Biology, and Society* (pp. 589–619). New York: Oxford Handbooks.

Schahbasi, A., Huber, S., & Fieder, M. (2021). Factors affecting attitudes toward migrants – an evolutionary approach. *American Journal of Human Biology*, 33(1), e23435.

Schwartz, C. R., & Gonalons-Pons, P. (2016). Trends in relative earnings and marital dissolution: Are wives who outearn their husbands still more likely to divorce? *RSF: The Russell Sage Foundation Journal of the Social Sciences*, 2(4), 218–236.

Smits, J. (2003). Social closure among the higher educated: Trends in educational homogamy in 55 countries. *Social Science Research*, 32(2), 251–277.

van Bavel, J. (2012). The reversal of gender inequality in education, union formation and fertility in Europe. *Vienna Yearbook of Population Research*, 127–154.

Vilas, R., Ceballos, F. C., Al-Soufi, L., González-García, R., Moreno, C., Moreno, M., ... & Álvarez, G. (2019). Is the "Habsburg jaw" related to inbreeding? *Annals of Human Biology*, 46(7–8), 553–561.

Whitmeyer, J. M. (1997). Endogamy as a basis for ethnic behavior. *Sociological Theory*, 15(2), 162–178.

10 Not so weird after all

Genesis 22:17 – I will surely bless you and make your descendants as numerous as the stars in the sky and as the sand on the seashore.
Quran 18:46 – Wealth and children are an ornament of the life of the world.

Evolutionary biology predicts a positive relationship between social status and number of offspring for humans, as is true in all social species. In this book we have seen evidence from a great many preindustrial societies past and present, from the simplest foraging societies to the most complex and hierarchical agricultural societies, that the highest status men and women in those societies with the best access to social and material resources do indeed have more children, on average, than others. Not only do higher-status people tend to have more children, but the quotes above from the Bible and the Quran remind us that in many preindustrial societies, numerous children are considered a blessing.

In the past, the highest status men in particular in these societies sometimes had a score or more children, a feat rarely accomplished by a woman. In fact in the large, agrarian despotisms of the past, male rulers could have multiple wives and/or concubines and sometimes hundreds of offspring. The man with the highest number of children on record, Moulay Ismail the Bloodthirsty of Morocco, sired more than 800 children. No woman could possibly match that. This sex difference is also consistent with theory from evolutionary biology that predicts a stronger relationship between status and fertility for men than for women, given women's evolved characteristics: their shorter reproductive time frames, their inability to have more than one or two children every year, combined with greater female biological investment in offspring. This consistency of theory and evidence suggests that humans share some characteristics with other social species, and the theory of evolutionary biology as applied to social species (sociobiology) is useful in studying humans as it is in studying other social species.

Yet the demographic transition that began in Europe in the 19th century seemingly changed everything. Families became small, and the first families to limit their family size were the elites – educated women married to educated

DOI: 10.4324/9781003463320-10

104   *Not so weird after all*

men in the professional, managerial, and other white-collar occupations of the new industrialized, market economies. The same thing has happened in every other demographic transition that has occurred – including the completed transitions in East Asia and China, for example – as well as demographic transitions that are currently occurring all over the world, including in the Middle East, Southeast Asia, and Africa. Well-educated women, in particular, are likely to have few or no children at all. For men, the negative effect of education on fertility is typically smaller than it is for women because education is often a precursor to a high-status, well-paying job, and in most countries such men are attractive as husbands.

This inversion of the relationship between status (as measured by education) and fertility in the new modern industrial societies of the 20th and 21st centuries is one of the phenomena that has led to people in these societies being labeled "the weirdest people in the world" – the people of Western, educated, industrialized, democratic nations (Henrich et al. 2010). By this view modern humans are part of a brave new world of people very different from people in preindustrial societies, and the fertility behavior of modern humans can no longer be explained by the predictions of sociobiology.

In this book we have argued that this assessment is premature. Societies developing from primarily agricultural societies to societies where most people work outside of agriculture and in industrial or service occupations are in transition. Everything in life is becoming different from what it was. Most people have gone from living and farming in small villages to living in cities and working in offices and factories, often in the time span of a generation or less. It takes individuals, populations, and cultures time to adjust to the profound new realities of a modern mass society. When we examine stable, post-transition societies in Europe, America, the former European colonies, and also East Asia, the evidence is clear that the relationship between status and fertility is changing and reverting to its former positive relationship. If social status is measured as personal income, arguably the most salient measure of status in modern societies, for men it has already changed. As we have seen, there is abundant evidence that in all stable, rich societies, high-income men are more likely to be married and have children, while low-income men are more likely to remain unmarried and childless, so there is a clear positive relationship between personal income and the number of children for men. For women the inverted relationship between personal income and fertility by and large remains. But in countries where the difficulties of combining work outside of the home with childbearing have been ameliorated by an extensive welfare state, such as in modern-day Sweden, there is evidence that the negative relationship between income and fertility for women has changed and is now positive in the more recent birth cohorts of women.

The positive relationship between status and fertility is clear only for income, not education, which remains negatively associated with fertility for men and women in most societies. Most of this is because of the years

Not so weird after all   105

required to obtain an education, and the fact that people tend to delay having children until after they have finished their education. Yet even this negative relationship between education and fertility seems to be changing for recent cohorts in the welfare states of Scandinavia and even in the very different societies of East Asia. Further, because education is positively associated with income and income is positively associated with fertility for men, everywhere the negative relationship between education and fertility is more muted for men than it is for women.

In our examination of the relationship between status and fertility in modern societies, we have measured status primarily using education, personal income, or household income, and often our measures of fertility rely on measures of female fertility alone. We use these measures because this is how researchers typically measure status and fertility in modern societies, and this is what is available in extant data sources. Yet for the examination of the relationship between status and fertility, arguably personal income takes precedence over education as a measure of individual status, as education can be seen as primarily a means to income, and income is clearly the more proximate measure of the resources necessary for childbearing and childraising. Yet because of sex differences in the tradeoffs involved in income earning and fertility in modern societies, the influence of personal income on fertility differs for men and women as we have seen. There is an urgent need for more research on the relationship between personal income and fertility and how this differs by sex. There is also a need for more research at the individual level on the determinants of male fertility, not just female fertility.

As we saw in Chapter 3, there are many other bases of social status that differ in importance depending on the type of society. In societies in the past, religious behavior has been an important means by which social status was granted and maintained. Religious activities, including participation in costly rituals, were an important way to gain or legitimize status in preindustrial societies, and thus were likely positively associated with fertility in the past. Given that all religions deal with morality and personal relationships including the family, it is not surprising that religiosity and religious behavior continue to be related to fertility. As we saw in Chapter 9, in modern societies religious people tend to have more children than less religious people. An important mechanism for this is religious homogamy – people of the same religion marrying each other – as religiously homogamous individuals also tend to have more children than nonhomogamous individuals. Today educational homogamy mimics to some extent the religious homogamy of yesterday, and like religious homogamy also has fertility consequences as we saw in Chapter 9. Given that there is evidence that these factors – education, personal income, and religiosity – have overlapping genetic bases, it is reasonable to wonder if in modern societies there is ongoing selection (either negative or positive) on those genetic polymorphisms involved with education, income, and religiosity. Yet, it is difficult to draw conclusions about

106 Not so weird after all

this, given the small amount of time humans have lived in rich modern societies. Only the genomes of the future will tell.

These recent findings from modern developed societies not only give support to theory from evolutionary biology, but they also suggest that modern humans are not as different from people in preindustrial societies or indeed from other social species as many like to think. Modern people are not so weird after all. Applications of evolutionary biology to humans are always controversial, as the reaction to Darwin's *The origin of species* in the 19th century and the negative response to E. O. Wilson's *Sociobiology* in the 1970s clearly demonstrate. Yet the relationship between status and fertility has no negative moral implications. In fact, the reemerging positive relationship between status and fertility underlines the similarity between people in all societies. By reminding us of this similarity it can serve to buttress ideas of human equality and further both humanitarian goals and the extension of human rights to all. In modern societies, if one of our goals is to ensure that the blessings of fertility and family life are spread equitably, fully understanding the relationship between status and fertility can help policy makers more adequately attain that goal.

Reference

Henrich, J., Heine, S. J., & Norenzayan, A. (2010). The weirdest people in the world? *Behavioral and Brain Sciences*, 33(2–3), 61–83.

Index

abandonment of children 9
Abma, J. C. 83
abortion 56, 63
Aché of Paraguay 30, 35
adaptive heritability of height and size 17
adaptive strategies 49, 85, 93
additional matings 10, 11; *see also* polygyny
Africa 66–69, 72
Agbaglo, E. 72
age: age (mother's) of first birth 16, 51, 52, 72, 73, 78, 79, 86–87, 99, 105; children of older fathers 16; correlation with beauty 19–20; limitation on women's fertility 11; men prefer younger women 11; older age and status 15–16; older men positively associated with desirability 11; social status 15–16; status increases with 11; youth preference 11–12, 15–16, 19–20
agrarian/agricultural societies 20–23, 35–39
Alcock, J. 6, 7
Alcorta, C. S. 93
Alexander, R. D. 84
Alexei Nikolaevich, Tsarevich 97
alliance building 18, 32–33
Altmann, S. A. 36
American General Social Survey xiii
Andersson, G. 79
Angrist, J. 72
Apostolou, M. 12
arbiter roles 34
archaeological records 30
archeogenetics 38
aristocracy 21; *see also* elite status; ruling classes

Arslan, R. C. 16
Ashura feast of Shia 18
Ashurst, H. 71
Atoh, M. 55, 56, 57, 58
Atran, S. 93
Australia 30, 52, 96
Ausubel, J. 11, 16

baby boom (post WWII) 49, 56
Babylonians 37
Bakharwal 32
Balaresque, Patricia 38
Banerjee, K. 41
Bangladesh 71
Banister, J. 60
Barclay, K. 82
Barrett, L. 18
Barthold, J. A. 83
Bateman, A. J. 10
Bateman's principle 5, 35
Beauchamp, J. P. 52, 86
Beaujouan, E. 79
beauty and social status 19–20
Becker, G. S. 72
Belgium 79
Bengtsson, T. 39
Betzig, L. 1, 33, 34, 35, 36, 37
Bhalotra, S. R. 48
Bible 95, 103
big gods 36, 37, 94
"big man"/chiefs 20
bilateral descent 31
biobank studies 85
biological resources 8–9
biparental investment 8
Bird, R. B. 84
blind process, evolution is 5
Blume, M. 95
body size/weight 16–18

108   *Index*

Boehm, C. 20
Bolivia 35
Bongaarts, J. 66, 67, 70, 71, 72
Boone, J. L. 41
Bora, J. K. 71
Borgerhoff Mulder, M. 1, 32
Borgia, G. 7
bowerbirds 7
Boyer, P. 93
brain size 21
Brazil 1, 32, 35, 73, 95
breastfeeding 8–9
"bridal suitors" 33
bride price 38
Bronfenbrenner, M. 56
Brooks, R. 7
Brown, J. R. 98
Bruch, E. E. 11
Brzozowska, Z. 79, 80
burial mounds 22–23
Buss, D. M. 74
Butz, W. P. 83
by-product theories of evolution 93

Callaway, E. 38
Campbell, A. 17
Canada 39, 50, 52
Caribbean 32, 35
caring for children and sexual selection 9
Casimir, M. J. 32
caste systems 23, 41
casual sex 10
Catchpole, C. K. 7
Ceballos, F. C. 96, 97
Celts 22, 38
census data 2, 56, 62, 73, 79, 80, 82, 84, 98
Cesarini, D. 82
Chagnon, N. A. 1, 32, 33, 34, 96
Chand, R. 22
Chang, M. C. 58, 59
Chen, H. 59
Chen, J. 61, 62
Chen, Y. H. 59
child mortality rates 47–48, 56, 59, 67
childlessness: China 62; contemporary transitioning societies 73, 74; East Asia 55, 57, 60; educational homogamy 99; and income levels 83, 104; post-transition societies 79–80; and women's employment 81–82
Chile 71, 73

China 38, 39, 41, 55, 60–64, 77
Chinese Family Panel Studies (CFPS) 61
choosiness in selecting a mate 10–11
clans 31
Clark, D. W. 96, 97
Clark, G. 18, 23, 38, 85
Clark and Hatfield experiment 10
"club law" 34
Coale, A. J. 48, 49
code of Hammurabi 36
cognitive abilities 18, 93
combat/fighting 16–17, 33, 34, 36
Commodus (son of Emperor Marcus Aurelius) 37
competition 7, 8, 16–18, 84
concubinage 37
Copper Eskimos 34
Corker, J. 72
costly signaling 7, 18–19, 93
courtship rituals 7
Crusades 19
"cult of the sun" 37
cultural complexity measures 31, 32

Dahomey empire 36
Danner, J. E. 15
Darwin, Charles 5, 33, 106
daughters, killing of 41, 63
Dawkins, Richard 1
Day, F. R. 92
De la Croix, D. 36
De la Vega, G. 37
definition of social status 2–3
delaying/postponement of first birth 51, 52, 72, 73, 78, 79, 86–87, 99, 105
Delehanty, D. 8
demographic transition: contemporary transitioning societies 66–76; East Asia 55–65; Europe and America 39, 47–54, 103–104; negative status-fertility relationship 2, 3
despotic cultures 33–34, 35–39
Diamond, J. 7
Dickemann, M. 41
Dinkel, R. M. 51
disease prevention/control 48, 56
displays of fighting ability 16–17
"divine father" 37
divorce 81, 82, 99
DNA (deoxyribonucleic acid) 5
dominance 16
D'Onofrio, B. D. 16
Dribe, M. 39, 50, 51, 52

Index 109

Drioui, C. 71
Dunbar, Robin 21, 38, 97
Dylan, Bob xiv
Dyson, T. 66

East Asia 55–65, 79, 80, 87, 105
education: changing relationship
  between education and fertility
  79; childlessness 79–80; China 61;
  educational homogamy 97–99;
  female fertility 59–60, 61–62, 79–80,
  86, 104; genetics 51–52, 86; and
  income 81, 99, 105; and likelihood of
  marriage 58, 72; male fertility 57, 59,
  60, 63, 64, 80, 86, 104; and marriage
  58, 72, 81; as measure of status 78;
  postponement of fertility 79, 87, 99,
  105; post-transition societies 78–81;
  relationship between education and
  fertility 51–52, 57–58, 59–60, 61–63,
  67, 71–72; religion 93; and religion
  93; required for substantial income
  78; U-shaped education-fertility
  curves 79, 80, 87
egalitarian societies 31
eggs and sperm 8–9
Egypt 96
elephant seals 16
elite status: "big man"/chiefs 20; female
  fertility 39; inverse relationship
  with fertility 77; kin marriage 97;
  monarchy and aristocracy 21;
  Norman Conquest 38; polygyny
  36–37; religious rituals 19; sources of
  1; unmarried/unpartnered women 41
employment status 52, 58, 60, 104;
  see also occupational status
Endler, J. A. 7
endogamy 21, 23, 95–100
Engelhardt, H. 79, 80
England 38, 48, 80, 81, 82
Enos, R. D. 98
Enríquez Varas, P. J. 71, 73
Esteve, A. 99
Ethiopia 72
evolutionary escalating loops 7
evolutionary theory 1, 5–14, 36, 77,
  84–85, 93, 103, 106
expression quantitative trait loci studies
  (eQTL) 85

Fairbairn, D. J. 17
faithfulness 11–12

family groups 23
fathers *see* male fertility
Fauve-Chamoux, A. 51
female fertility: education 59–60, 61–62,
  79–80, 86, 104; employment 52,
  81–82, 104; female hypogamy 99;
  income 83, 99–100, 104; inverse
  relationship between education and
  fertility 51–52; limited window 9,
  11, 87, 103; long working hours 78;
  preindustrial societies 34–35; social
  status 78
females: age and social status 16; age
  of first birth 51; agrarian societies
  39–41; beauty and social status
  19–20; benefits of polygyny for 36;
  choosiness in selecting a mate 10–11;
  control over sexual behaviour of 23;
  female fidelity 33; female infanticide
  41; female investment in offspring
  8–9; fights over 33; fixed biological
  investment in children 8–9; height
  and size 18; high-status females
  39; inverse relationship between
  education and fertility 51–52;
  men choosing high status women
  11; preference for good hunters
  32; social status 15; unmarried/
  unpartnered women 41, 51, 56–57,
  59, 62, 72
Feng, W. 38, 39
Fertile Crescent 37
fertility, measuring 2–3
fidelity 11–12, 33
Fieder, M. 16, 19, 22, 25, 34, 36, 52,
  72, 73, 78, 80, 81, 82, 83, 84, 85, 86,
  92, 93, 95, 96, 97, 98, 99
fights/violence 16–17, 33, 34
Finland 79, 80, 81, 82, 85
Fisher's principle 8
fitness 5, 12, 33, 38, 84
Flap, H. 98
Fleisher, B. M. 83
Flinn, M. 32, 35
Florence 41
forager societies 30–31, 32
Fox, R. 95, 96, 98
France 41, 49, 52, 55, 79
Freedman, D. S. 83
Freedman, R. 61, 62
free-riders 21
Frejka, T. 83
friendship strategies 18

110 *Index*

General Social Survey of China 63
genetics: correlates of status and
   fertility 4; despotic cultures 38; DNA
   (deoxyribonucleic acid) 5; education
   51–52, 86; genetic drift 6; genetic kin
   involvement in mate selection 12;
   in-group preferences 95–96;
   homogamy 97; income 85; natural
   selection 5–6; post-transition societies
   85–87; religion 92–93
Genghis Khan 38
genomic data 16, 85, 96
Germany 38, 77, 79, 80
Ghana 72
Ghaznavi, C. 57, 58
Gibson, M. A. 36
Gini coefficient 21–22
"god-kings" 36, 37
Gonalons-Pons, P. 99
Goodman, A. 81
grave goods 23
group size 21, 97
Guo, J. 61, 62
guppies 7
Guzzo, K. B. 78, 80
GWA studies 92

Habakkuk, H. J. 38
Habsburg, House of 23–26, 94, 97
Hackett, C. 95
Hadza 30–32, 33, 34
Hailemariam, A. 72
Hallstatt culture 22
Hamilton, William 5, 12, 34
handicap principle 7
harems 36
Hayford, S. R. 78, 80
health, indicators of 18
Heaton, T. B. 95
height and social status 16–18
hemophilia 97
Henrich, J. 34, 93, 104
herders 32
heritable traits 5, 6, 17, 85, 97
heterogamy 96
Hill, K. 30, 49
Hill, W. D. 18, 85
Hinduism 18
Hodgson, D. 66, 67, 70, 71, 72
homogamy 3, 95–100, 105
homozygosity 96
Hopcroft, Rosemary L. 15, 40, 73, 74,
   80, 81, 82, 83, 99

horticultural societies 20–21, 32–34
House of Habsburg 23–26, 94, 97
House of Welf 97
Houses of the Chosen Women 36
Hrdy, S. B. 41
Huber, S. 16, 19, 22, 25, 36, 52, 73, 78,
   80, 81, 82, 83, 84, 85, 86, 92, 93, 95,
   97, 98, 99
Hudde, A. 79, 80
Hughes, A. L. 38
hunting ability 31, 32
hunting and gathering 4, 12, 17, 18,
   19–20, 30–32
Hurtado, A. M. 30
Hutterites 39
hypergamy 99
Hyytinen, A. 85

illegitimate children 37–38, 57, 63, 81
inbreeding 37, 96–97
Inca Empire 36–37
inclusive fitness theory 5, 12, 33
income: contemporary transitioning
   societies 72–73; and education 81,
   99, 105; and fertility within couples
   83–84; genetics 85; husband's income
   and wife's number of children 83–84;
   income measures of social status
   52–53, 77–78, 105; number of
   children 2; positive relationship with
   male fertility xiii, 58, 60, 63, 81–84,
   100, 104; post-transition societies
   81–83; probability of marriage 81,
   82; relationship with number of
   children 58, 60, 63, 81–84, 100,
   104; reverse J-shaped income-fertility
   curves 52; U-shaped income-fertility
   curves 52; wife's versus husband's
   and effect on number of children 74,
   83–84
incomes (national/GDP) 56, 67, 79
India 18, 23, 32, 41, 71
Indian National Family Health Survey
   71
indirect competition for mates 17–18
industrial societies 26, 47–54, 55–56,
   58, 60
inequality 21–22, 26, 31, 35, 36, 37, 94
infant mortality rates 47–48, 56, 59
infanticide 41
infectious disease prevention 48, 56
inheritance of mother's social status 37
inherited property/wealth 21, 22, 26, 37

Index 111

intelligence 18–19, 85
intergenerational transmission of social status 26, 86
intergenerational wealth transmission 22
intersexual selection 6, 7
intrasexual selection 6–7
inverse relationship between education and fertility 51–52
investment in offspring 7, 8–9
IPUMS international 73
Iran 35
Ireland 49
Irons, W. 1, 84
Islam 18, 34
Ismail the Bloodthirsty of Morocco 9, 103
Israel 74, 84
Italy 41

Jæeger, M. M. 18, 20
Jalovaara, M. 79, 80, 81
Japan 39, 41, 55–58, 77
Jenness, D. 34
Jones, G. W. 56, 58, 59, 60, 72
Jones, J. H. 84
Jones, M. B. 41

Kalmijn, M. 98
Kaplan, H. 30, 49
Kaptijn, R. 80
Kemp, D. J. 7
Kenya 1, 32, 35
"Khans" 38
kill rates 32, 33
Kim, D. S. 60
kin, numbers of 32, 33
kin marriage 37, 96–97, 98
kin networks 12, 34, 36, 96
kin selection 33
kinship cooperation 33, 34
Kipsigis 1, 32, 35
Koenig, L. B. 92
Kolk, M. 81, 82, 83, 85, 87, 100
Kong, A. 16, 52, 86
Korea 59–60, 77
koseki law (Family Registration System Law, Japan) 56
Koupil, I. 81, 82
Kravdal, Ø. 79, 81
Krummhörn farmers 38
Kruuk, L. E. 17
"Kurfürsten" (princeps elector imperii) 24
Kurosu, S. 39

land ownership: female fertility 35, 39; horticultural societies 21; kin marriage 96; lack of data on 74; and number of children 32, 38; religion 19; and status 1, 15
Lappegård, T. 80, 81
large gametes 8
Latin America 71, 73
life expectancy 48, 55, 56, 60
Lim, Sojung 59, 60
Litchfield, R. B. 41
Liu, T. C. 58
Livermore, H. V. 37
livestock ownerships 1; see also pig ownership
Livi-Bacci, M. 50
long working hours 78
long-term partners 11–12
lottery wins 82
low fertility societies 2, 3

Mace, R. 36, 49
Majolo, B. 16
male fertility: age of fatherhood 16; contemporary transitioning societies 73; demographic transition 50; education 57, 59, 60, 63, 64, 80, 86, 104; higher social status and greater number of offspring 1–2; lack of data on xiii, 51; lack of focus on 3; limted fixed investment in children 8, 9; need for more research 105; parental investment theory 8–9, 11; paternity uncertainty 11–12, 15, 33; positive relationship with income xiii, 58, 60, 63, 81–84, 100, 104; social status 78
Malenfant, R. M. 17
males: age and social status 16; beauty and social status 19–20; control of women 23, 33, 41; height and size 16–18; high-status males 23; religious rituals 18–19; social status 15, 30; unmarried/unpartnered men 34, 35, 36, 38, 51, 58, 59, 60, 104
Maloney, T. N. 50, 52
Maori 34
Mariani, F. 36
Marlowe, Frank M. 30–32
marriage: age of 49; delaying 52, 56–57, 58, 62; and education 58, 72, 81; endogamy 21, 23, 95–100; Hadza 31–32; homogamy 95–100; and income levels 81, 82; marital fertility

112 Index

rate measures 39; marriage networks 33; matrimonial expenditures 96; monogamy 31, 32, 34, 35, 36, 37; politics 26; polygyny 16, 31–39; property/wealth 38; religious marriage rules 95; serial monogamy 31–32, 34, 35–36
Martin, T. C. 71
Martinez, G. M. 83
mate preferences 9–13
maternal inheritance 37
mates, finding 6–13
maximal group size 21, 97
Mazur, A. 18
Mbuti Pygmies 31
McCann, T. S. 16
medal of honor 19
medical science 48
Meisenberg, G. 93
Melanesia 20
menopause 32
mentalizing 93
Meriam 30
Meyer, H. E. 18
middle classes 50
Middle East 71, 73
MIDUS twin study 85
Mijs, J. J. 98
Miller, G. 18, 19
Mills, M. 6, 72
Mokyr, J. 48
monarchs 21, 97; see also ruling classes
Mongols 38
monogamy 31, 32, 34, 35, 36, 37
Moore, F. 52
Mormons 95
mortality rates 47–48, 56, 58, 59, 60
Most Prolific Mother Ever 9
Moulay Ismail the Bloodthirsty 9, 103
Mueller, U. 18
Mulder, M. B. 22, 36
murder rates 31, 32
Murdoch, G. P. 31, 32
Murphy, M. 66

Nathan, M. 73
National Longitudinal Survey of Youth (NLSY79) 80, 81
natural selection 5–6
neo-cortex size 21
Netherlands 38, 39, 80
Nettle, D. 18, 80, 81, 82
New Zealand 34

Newman, M. E. J. 11
Nisén, J. 79, 80, 81, 82
Norenzayan, A. 92, 93, 94
Norse 37–38
Norway 18, 50, 52, 79, 80, 81, 82
nuns 41

O'Bryan, S. 56
occupational status: contemporary transitioning societies 73; demographic transition 50–51, 60; and education 80; female employment and fertility 52; as measure of status 21, 23, 26, 78; and property/wealth 78; women's as husband's 39, 50
Ogawa, N. 58
older age and status 15–16
"one child policy" (China) 61, 63
One-per-Thousand Survey 61
ornaments/signaling 7–8; see also costly signaling
outside-of-marriage childbearing 37–38, 57, 63, 81

Papua New Guinea 32, 35
parental investment theory 5, 8–9, 11, 17–18
paternity uncertainty 11–12, 15, 33
patrilineages 33
Pawlowski, B. 18
peacocks 7
Petersen, W. 38, 51
phalaropes 8
pig ownership 32, 35
Piotrowski, M. 57, 58
Pisanski, K. 18
pleiotropic loci 6
Plomin, R. 18, 85
plow agriculture 21
polar bears 17
Pollet, T. V. 80, 81, 82
polygenic traits 6, 86
polygyny 16, 31–39
Polynesia 20
population growth 48–49, 66–67
population shrinkage 77, 84
Portugal 41
postponement of first birth 51, 52, 72, 73, 78, 79, 86–87, 99, 105
post-transition societies 77–91, 104
predisposition does not equal behavior 10
pregnancy and lactation 8–9
preindustrial societies 1, 2, 30–46

Index 113

primates 16, 21
Privilegium maius 24
probate data studies 38
Prokosch, M. D. 18
property/wealth: kin marriage 96–97;
 later births 39; less of a predictor
 of fertility than income 82–83; and
 number of children 38; post-transition
 societies 78, 81–83; as prerequisite for
 marriage 63; property rights 21
pro-sociality 93–94
prostitution 10
Provost, C. 31, 32
public health 48

Quebec 39
Quran 95, 103

race 83, 96
Rao, A. 32
Rapley, E. 41
Raymo, J. M. 57, 60
red deer 6–7, 17
relative fitness 84
Relethford, J. H. 6, 96
religion: costly signaling 18–19; despotic
 cultures 37; and education 93; and
 fertility 71; homogamy 3; marriage
 rules 95; religious leaders 21, 23;
 social rules 36; social status 21,
 92–95, 105
replacement fertility levels 49, 55, 60,
 71, 77
"restitution by plunder" 34
revenge 32–33, 34
reverse J-shaped income-fertility curves 52
Reynolds, J. D. 7
Rhodes, G. 83
Rindfuss, R. R. 79, 81
rituals 32–33
Roe, E. L. 98
Rollides 37–38
Roman Empire 24, 37, 94
Romania 79
Rønsen, M. 80, 81
Roser, M. 55
Rostworowski de Diez Canseco, M. 37
Rudolf IV, Emperor 23–24
ruling classes 23, 36, 37, 38
running speed 17
rural/urban differences in fertility rates
 58, 61–62, 67
Rusch, H. 19

Salem, R. 96
Sanderson, S. K. 93
Santtila, P. 63
Scandinavia 79–80, 81, 83, 87, 105
Scania 39, 51
Schahbasi, A. 36, 97
Scheidel, W. 21, 22, 35, 36, 37
Schneider, D. 83
Schwartz, C. R. 99
Scotland 52
Selmer, R. 18
Semana Santa processions 18
serial monogamy 31–32, 34, 35–36
sex ratios in the population 8
sexual divisions of labor 31
sexual selection 6–13, 17
Shackelford, T. K. 74
Shah, S. 96
Sheehan, O. 36
Shenk, M. K. 84
Shinbone clan 34
Shirahase, S. 57
Siberia 30
siblings 33, 37
signaling for a mate 7; *see also* costly
 signaling
Silventoinen, K. 17
size (body) 16–18
Skirbekk, V. 51, 55, 66, 67, 71, 73
slavery 37
small gods 93
Smith, E. A. 30
Smits, J. 98
Smrcka, V. 23
Smuts, B. 15, 23
Sobotka, T. 55, 57, 59
social and cultural contexts 10
social class 50, 52–53; *see also* ruling
 classes
social hierarchies 36–37
social rules 12, 36, 37
social status: agricultural societies
 20–23; burial mounds 22–23;
 correlated with more children
 in hunter-gatherer societies 30;
 education 98; female status and
 fertility 34–35; and fertility 12; high
 status and greater number of offspring
 1, 2; high status and low numbers of
 offspring 2; high status as reason for
 choosing a mate 10–11; high-status
 females 39; high-status males 23;
 illegitimate children 37; industrial

114   *Index*

societies 26; inherited abilities 85; intergenerational transmission of 23–26, 86; polygyny as marker of 33; post-transition societies 77; preindustrial societies 30–46; as reason for choosing a mate 10–12; relative status between spouses 63; religion 92–95; sex-based 26; sources of 15–29; universal markers of status 15; *see also* occupational status
sociobiology 1–2, 5, 103, 106
"someone who has killed" status 32, 33
son preference 41, 63
songs 15
Sorokowski, P. 32, 35
Sosis, R. 93
South Korea 59–60
Southeast Asia 71–72
"spare" children in high mortality environments 49
sparrows 15
sperm mutations 16
Srivastava, S. K. 22
St Stephen's Cathedral, Vienna 24, 25
Stulp, G. 18, 81, 82, 83
Sumerians 37
surname studies 85–86
Sweden 39, 51, 52, 79, 80, 81, 82, 85, 87, 99–100, 104
Switzerland 49

tactical skill 18
Taiwan 58–59, 77
Tanzania 30–31
Thaipusam 18–19
theory of mind 93
Thornhill, N. W. 37
Thornton, A. 83
1000 Genomes Project 16
Tierra del Fuego 34
total fertility rates (TFRs): contemporary transitioning societies 66–67, 71, 72; data table 68–69; East Asia 56, 58, 59, 61–62; Europe and America 49; graph 70; occupational status 73; post-transition societies 77; Southeast Asia 72
Treadway, R. 49
tribal societies 32–34, 94, 98
Trinidad 32
Trivers, Robert 5, 7, 8

Tsimane 35
Tsuya, N. O. 39, 58
Turke, P. W. 84
twin studies 85, 92

UK 38, 48, 80, 81, 82
UN Population Division 70
universal markers of status 15
unmarried/unpartnered men 34, 35, 36, 38, 51, 58, 59, 60, 104
unmarried/unpartnered women 41, 51, 56–57, 59, 62, 72
Unokai ("someone who has killed") 33
urban/rural differences in fertility rates 58, 61–62, 67
Uruguay 73
US (United States): demographic transition 49, 50, 51, 52; education and fertility 80; educational homogamy 99; husband's income and wife's number of children 83–84; income, wealth and fertility 81; life expectancy 48; positive relationship between male fertility and income 82; religiosity 92; U.S. Census data 2, 80, 82, 98; war heroism as costly signaling 19
U-shaped education-fertility curves 79, 80, 87
U-shaped income-fertility curves 52
Utah 52

Van Bavel, J. 79, 99
van der Vaart, S. A. 23
Vassilyev, Feodor 9
Venezuela 1, 32, 35, 73
Verweij, R. M. 80, 81, 83
Vézina, H. 39
Vilas, R. 97
Vining, D. R. 2, 84
Voland, E. 38
von Rueden, C. 83
von Stumm, S. 85

Walder, A. G. 61
Wang, R. J. 16
war heroism as costly signaling 19
Ward, M. P. 83
warrior status 15, 23
Weeden, J. 81, 82, 83
Welf, House of 97

Index 115

welfare state 104, 105
Westoff, C. F. 51
whales 15
Whitmeyer, J. M. 95
widow suicide 41
widows, remarriage of 41
William the Conqueror 37–38
Wilson, E. O. 1, 106
Wilson's phalaropes 8
Wisconsin Longitudinal Study 80, 81, 82, 92
women *see* female fertility
Wood, J. 79
working classes 50
World Fertility Survey 71

Xavante 35
Xie, Y. 62, 63
Xu, Q. 61, 63

Yali 32, 35
Yanomami 1, 20, 32–34, 35, 96
Yeung, W. J. J. 72
Yomut Turkmen 1, 35
Yoo, Sam Hyun 59–60
youth 11–12, 15–16, 19–20
Yu, J. 62, 63

Zahavi, A. 7
Zhang, Y. 63
Ziker, J. P. 30

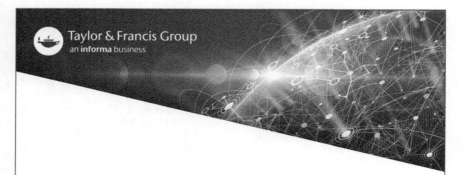